THE UNIVERSITY OF MICHIGAN
CENTER FOR SOUTH AND SOUTHEAST ASIAN STUDIES

MICHIGAN PAPERS ON SOUTH AND SOUTHEAST ASIA

Ann Arbor, Michigan

THE SOCIALIZATION OF FAMILY SIZE VALUES:

YOUTH AND FAMILY PLANNING

IN AN INDIAN VILLAGE

Thomas Poffenberger
in association with
Kim Sebaly

Ann Arbor
Center for South and Southeast Asian Studies
The University of Michigan
1976

Michigan Papers on South and Southeast Asia, 12

Library of Congress Catalog Card Number 76-53996

International Standard Book Number 0-89148-012-9

Copyright

1976

by

Center for South and Southeast Asian Studies

The University of Michigan

Table of Contents

Tables

Preface

The population projections for India are based on the probability that the large cohorts of youth entering the reproductive age will have relatively large families. With this concern in mind, population education programs designed to reduce the number of children young people have were suggested some years ago. One such program was established at the University of Baroda, India, and long-term research was contemplated both to provide information for implementing a program in Gujarat State as well as to determine its effect. The project did not develop as planned. However, data were available from a small pilot project which was conducted in preparation for the larger study. While some of the data have been made available in mimeographed form (Poffenberger and Sebaly, 1971), it was never completed as a monograph. There are perhaps two justifications for doing so now. First, there continues to be interest in population education. In some developing countries large programs have been established and others are in various stages of development and implementation.

Most population education programs have been based on the assumption that children at all ages can learn about population related matters in school which will modify later fertility behavior. Yet, as is illustrated in this monograph, the most important learning regarding fertility behavior may be unrelated to any school activity and an understanding of the nature of this learning can be useful to program planners.

The present research approaches the problem from the standpoint of the socialization of youth. Socialization is not only the preparation of youth to perform traditional roles but also the teaching of new roles which are necessary as a result of changes affecting the society. It is the consistency with which roles are performed from one generation to the next that maintains established social structure and much has been made of the need to change the structure of peasant societies if fertility is to be changed. A focus on role socialization may help assess the extent to which social change is taking place.

A second reason for publishing the data has to do with the issue of fertility motives among the rural poor. Old questions were raised again at the 1974 Bucharest World Population Conference regarding the significance of government-directed family planning programs compared to economic development as a means of reducing fertility rates.

The need for increasing the welfare of the peasant in developing countries can hardly be stated in strong enough terms. There are clearly gross economic inequalities and these are illustrated in the present research. In spite of the attempts to change land tenure conditions in many countries, the rural landowning elites often continue to hire landless peasants for poverty wages. The agricultural technologies of the 1960's require capital, so those who already have money are in the best position to take advantage of such advances. In the area where this research was conducted, the assistance that has been given has tended to increase rather than decrease the distance between rich and poor agriculturists in the same villages.

Some at Bucharest stressed the point that poor people must have large families in order to survive and took the position that family planning programs not only cannot succeed but are not in the interests of the rural poor. In terms of India, Mamdani (1972) is perhaps the most frequently quoted proponent of this view. As a result of a study of a North Indian village, he concluded that the only hope of the rural poor to rise in economic status was to have more sons. Boulding (1973) in a review of the Mamdani report agreed. He said, "The message is very simple—nobody will restrict his family unless it pays to do so—and the brutal truth is that, especially for the poor in circumstances where some emigration is possible, big families pay.

Stycos (1964), in answer to both Mamdani and those with a similar position at Bucharest, pointed out that in the last 20 years or so, a large number of systematic studies have been conducted in Third World countries regarding attitudes toward family size. He summarizes these results by saying, "One common theme that comes out loud and clear from the most intensive research of recent years is that most poor people do not want large families. Much of the data, however, come from the so-called KAP (knowledge, attitude, practice) studies and it is the results of these surveys that have been questioned. Why, many ask, if people say they do not want large families, do they not behave in ways which would reduce family size?

Part of the apparent confusion is that many villagers are in a dilemma. They do indeed need children to survive but children can also complicate their survival. This dilemma has been discussed in a previous report recording adult attitudes and behavior in the same region (Poffenberger, 1975). The present monograph may give some additional feeling for how youth views the need for children as a result of changes affecting village life.

For both adults and young people, there was seldom one point of view held on any subject including fertility behavior. Some did believe that the only way to wealth was to have as many sons as possible. Others, however, felt that too many sons, as well as daughters, presented many problems and the costs were greater than the rewards. For most villagers there was a range of children they would prefer to have and this range had an upper limit. However, the methods available to them to avert births, for one reason or another, were difficult to accept and this has sometimes been confused with not wanting to limit family size. While large families continued to be important there were an increasing number of families where fertility limitation after several children was regarded as necessary to ease economic as well as other stresses. For some of these couples the desire not to have additional children was strong enough to overcome the fear of accepting an effective method.

The data are limited to interviews taken from all those attending the final year of a village secondary school on the days the study was conducted. Although they were a select group, we had the advantage of interviewing some of the more articulate village youths, and also that group included young people from very poor and middle income village families as well as from families of relative wealth. It is the stories of the poor that perhaps tell us the most about the complexities of the relationship between economic development and fertility. There is evidence that fertility among the poor may be declining, not because things are getting better but because things are getting worse. It is however important to again emphasize the variations in families that exist not only between groups but within groups in the same village. Too often village studies have given the impression that people in peasant societies are much the same and that information from a few informants provides a reliable base to judge the beliefs and behavior of the whole. Another question of validity can be justifiably raised. Even if one attempts to interview those with differing characteristics within the village, are we recording what the respondent, in an effort to please, thinks the interviewer wants to hear? In an attempt to permit the reader to empathize with each student as an individual as well as to judge the significance of the responses, the report provides relevent parts of what was said regarding the topic discussed in each section.

Acknowledgments

We wish to thank the many people at the University of Baroda who assisted in the conduct of this research. The project could not have been successfully completed without the generous support of the Vice-Chancellor, C. S. Patel; the Pro Vice-Chancellor, P. J. Madan; Dean D. M. Desai, Faculty of Education and Psychology; Dr. M. B. Buch, Director and B. P. Lulla, Program Director of the Center of Advanced Study in Education; former Dean of the Faculty of Social Work, G. G. Dadlani, Dean Indira Patel and Bihari Pandya. Also, Mrs. Amita Verma, Chairman of the Department of Child Development for her assistance over a number of years of research in the region. We would particularly like to thank Mrs. Varsha Anjaria, Lecturer, Faculty of Social Work at Baroda University, for her continued interest in the study and cooperation in returning to the village for additional interview information; also, Mr. D. C. Joshi, doctoral candidate of the Tata Institute of Social Science, who helped Mrs. Anjaria conduct the interviews with village students. We are deeply grateful to Richard Bennett from the University of Michigan who assisted in the field work, to Shri R. S. Patel, Headmaster of the Varnama secondary school, and the thirty-nine students who participated in the interviews.

Kim Sebaly directed the field work and assisted in the analysis of the data and in the preparation of the report. It was written by the senior author.

xii

The Eleventh Standard Students of Varna Village, 1969-70

The Interviewers...
and the Faculty

I. Background and Methodology

In the summer of 1968, as a part of the Baroda-Michigan program, a seminar was held at the University of Michigan regarding a collection of data that might be useful in planning the development of a population education division in the Faculty of Education at the University of Baroda in Gujarat State, India. The activities in the Faculty of Education in Baroda were to include community field work in both school and non-school programs, curriculum and material development, teacher training and research and evaluation.

Initial consideration of a large sample survey of students was regarded as premature without some preliminary information. As a result, it was decided to undertake a small study interviewing all the students in the Eleventh Standard, the final class of an Indian village secondary school, regarding a wide range of population and fertility knowledge, and attitudes concerning their families, the village and the country. The survey was to be largely concerned with the question of what it is like to grow up in a rapidly changing society, yet one still basically rural and traditional, but with increasing pressures of urbanization and industrialization being felt throughout the region.

The study was not designed to be quantitative. The purpose was to develop as much understanding as possible of the lives of a few students with the assumption that it might provide a basis for planning further research.

Our purpose in interviewing students from the Eleventh Standard was a practical one. The project required working with the teachers in the village school, in cooperation with the Faculty of Education at the University of Baroda, to develop an experimental population education program. Since the work was to be with students of this age we wanted to know how and what some of them were learning about population related matters. With this information we could proceed a bit more systematically.

In the spring and summer of 1969, two staff members from the University of Michigan supervised the field study while working at the University of Baroda with the Baroda-Michigan project. Varna village[1] was selected for study, which was a

1

part of the project's rural teacher-training program where rapport was well established. Two interviewers, a male and female, with previous village interviewing experience, were employed from the teaching staff of the Faculty of Social Work at the University of Baroda. The interviewers were proficient in Gujarati (the local language) and English. The interview schedule was translated into Gujarati, pretested and revised. Following a series of meetings with the village school administration there was some additional modification of the questions.

In all, 39 students were interviewed: 26 males and 13 females—the total attendance in the Eleventh Standard. The students were between 16 and 19 years of age. The modal age was 17 years. Six of the males and one female were married. Thirty-three of the students were from Varna village. Six students were males from three other villages, the most distant, three miles away.

The interviews were conducted daily before (afternoon) classes began, from June 15 to August 12, 1969, the beginning of the local school year. The interviewers were instructed to record the comments just as they were given by the students. Notes were taken in Gujarati to facilitate recall and recording of statements by the interviewers after the termination of each interview. There were no check lists. All questions were open-ended permitting maximum expression. Following each session, time was allowed for the interviewer to record comments, including his/her interpretation of the quality and validity of the student's responses. The latter was done because we were interested in the opinion of the interviewers regarding any responses that, in their judgment, might not have indicated the full extent of the student's knowledge or opinion. After the interviewers looked over each interview and made sure that statements were complete, they translated these into English. The translations were discussed with the two resident Michigan staff members to clarify interpretation of local terms and phrases.

The two interviewers did their interviewing and translating independently of each other. The range of responses for each question was virtually the same for the two interviewers. Also, the interview content was generally consistent with other data collected from nearby villages (Poffenberger, 1968, 1975; Anker, 1973; Poffenberger and Poffenberger, 1973).

The interviews were reviewed in a series of meetings at
the University of Michigan. Response groupings were derived
from those seminar discussions.

The Village

The village was located eight miles south of Baroda city,
near a trunk highway. It was a large village with a population of
3,268 in 1961. Of these, 1,734 (53 percent) were males and
1,534 (47 percent) were females. Of the males, 830 (49 percent)
and of the females, 411 (27 percent) were recorded as "literate
and educated" (Government of India Census, 1961, p. 34).

The majority of those employed were engaged in agri-
culture. Of the 1,019 village men listed as employed, 37 percent
were agricultural laborers. Nearly half as many women as men
were reported to be employed, and of these, 88 percent represented poorer families engaged in farm labor (Table 1).

The village had electricity, as did many villages in the
surrounding area. It had a post office, a primary school and the
higher secondary school which also served several smaller
villages nearby.

The village had a range of Hindu castes (jati) represented
from the highest to the lowest social status. The 1961 Census
reported that over two-thirds (69 percent) of the village population
were caste Hindus. Of the remainder, 12 percent were members
of Scheduled Castes and 19 percent were members of Scheduled
Tribes. Scheduled Castes were former "Untouchables" whose
inherited status related to a subgroup's involvement in performing
tasks such as removing dead animals from the village, sweeping,
leather work and other occupations regarded as ritually contam-
inating for in-caste Hindus. Scheduled Tribes were those persons
of aboriginal ancestry and the original inhabitants of the area.
Since the 1961 Census did not indicate caste names, an estimate
of the percentage of high and lower caste members was taken
from family names in village records. These records indicated
that about 30 percent of the villagers were members of higher
status castes while about 38 percent were from middle and lower
status castes.

Table 1

Occupational Classification for All Male
and Female Workers in Varna Village
(Adapted from:
Government of India Census, 1961, p. 68)

Occupation	Males		Females	
	N	Percent	N	Percent
Cultivator	371	37	10	2
Agricultural laborer	357	36	443	88
Household industry	44	4	16	3
Manufacturing other than household industry	105	10	25	5
Trade and commerce	25	2	0	0
Transport, storage and communication	31	3	0	0
Other services	86	8	10	2
Total workers	1019	100	504	100

Caste and Economic Groupings

There was a wide range in the reported annual income of the students' families, from Rs. 16,000[2] for a wealthy zamindar (landowner) to Rs. 500 or less for the families of day laborers representing the Scheduled Castes and Tribes.

The students could be divided into three groups: 27 from relatively high caste families, four from lower caste families and eight from Scheduled Caste families including one from a Scheduled Tribe.

For those high caste families without reported economic problems, the average yearly income for all members was about Rs. 6,500. Of the fourteen students in this group, ten of the fathers were farmer-landowners. The others were merchants and professionals.

There were thirteen high caste families where the students reported economic problems. For this group the average annual income was Rs. 2,600. Again, most of the fathers were farmer-landowners but the holdings were considerably smaller on the average than the more affluent families.

The average income for the four lower caste families was Rs. 1,325. Three of the fathers worked their own small land-holdings while one father served as a clerk in a local government office. One son worked in the city and another as a tailor in the village.

For the Scheduled Castes and Tribes, the average family income was Rs. 563. Most of these fathers worked as day laborers for village landowners and in most of these families the mother also worked for daily wages in the fields.

Most of the fathers of the sample, then, followed traditional agricultural occupations, in the higher and lower castes as farmers, and in the Scheduled Castes as day laborers for persons with large landholdings. However, it was also evident that increasing numbers of young men from all castes were attempting to obtain jobs in factories, mills and other forms of steady employment in the city.

Varna village was not necessarily representative of the region. Villages differ both in terms of wealth and the percent of various castes and communities which comprise the population. Neither were the students representative of the village. The high caste and the "untouchable" communities were over-represented in terms of enrollment, while the lower castes were under-represented, as were children with tribal backgrounds. Although the higher castes made up about 30 percent of the village population, over 50 percent of the male students and 100 percent of the female students were from higher caste families. Lower caste members who made up about 38 percent of the village population were under-represented in the school with only 15 percent of the male students from these families. There was only one boy in the class from a Bhil family yet this "tribal" group made up

Table 2

Population of Varna Village and Student Enrollment in Eleventh Standard by Caste Status

(Population figures are from the Government
of India Census, 1961, p. 34; estimates for
high castes and lower castes were taken
from village records.)

Caste Status	Total Village Population		Students Enrolled in Eleventh Standard			
			Males		Females	
	N	%	N	%	N	%
High Castes	1014	31	14	54	13	100
Lower Castes	1230	38	4	15	0	0
Scheduled Castes	388	12	7	27	0	0
Scheduled Tribes	636	19	1	4	0	0
Totals	3268	100	26	100	13	100

19 percent of the population. Of significance, however, was that those who had the lowest ascribed status, members of the Scheduled Castes (former "untouchables"), who made up 12 percent of the village population, were represented by 27 percent of the male student enrollment, in part because of the special educational benefits available to persons of this group, but more important, because of their increasing achievement orientation in recent years (Table 2). [3]

The sample students were also a select group in that they came from specific families which clearly valued education. For many low income families, the education of children was a significant sacrifice, even for those who had partial government support. Last, the high dropout rate in village schools was in part due to the inability of many boys and girls to pass the required course work. The fact that these students had made it to the Eleventh Standard indicated that they were probably more richly endowed than the average student with the attributes required to perform the kind of school work required. In the days the interviewers worked in the school, only 39 of the enrolled 49 students were present. Of the 39 students inter- viewed, one-third were girls. All but one of the girls enrolled were present while over a fourth of the boys enrolled were absent. This seemed largely because the girls represented only high caste families. Because of family work needs, lower status boys found it difficult to attend regularly.

While the select nature of the group of students studied has been stressed here, it should also be added that much of what was found does have general relevance to the local village youth and their families and to the Baroda area. The sample students were perhaps better able to express themselves than other village youth, but students from the various castes and communities were represented with extreme variations in economic status. The problems they talked about were obviously those of the entire village—and probably much of rural India.

The Secondary School

While primary schools through the Seventh Standard are supported and controlled by Gujarat State, secondary schools have been constructed and funded largely by local efforts. The secondary school in Varna village was financed by a local trust fund begun by wealthy village landowners. Donations to the school fund were frequently made at the time of marriages in the village and contributions were collected annually by a door-to- door canvass of village families. The school was well-supported financially by village families and it owned 13 acres of land which provided crops which were auctioned at each harvest. In addition to a small tuition and some government support, there was not only adequate money to run the school but enough had been put aside to plan a new building. The school was not only well- supported financially but given close attention by the high caste village leaders who made up a self-perpetuating sixteen-member board of trustees.

With the increasing stress on education in the area, a

secondary school in a village had become a sign of position as
well as providing the education believed to be needed for local
youth. This was indicated in the plans of many villages in the
area to begin secondary schools. The senior author talked to
the headman of one rather small village who said that he planned
to have a secondary school even though there was one less than
a mile away that was far more adequate than any his village
would be able to afford. His comments made clear the compe-
titive aspect of the desire for the school. Behind the desire lay
an economic factor. Villages as well as families in the region
could be clearly ranked on a scale from low to high status. A
major way of moving up in the hierarchy was to marry a
daughter into a village and family of higher status than one's
own. The size of the dowry the family of the bride paid depended
in part upon the hierarchical position of the village from which
she came. In recent years, with the increase in the importance
of education, the presence of a secondary school had become an
item to consider in the bartering process. Aside from the general
value of a secondary school, it had gained importance specifically
in terms of the education of girls. With the increasing level of
education of high caste boys, there was a gradual increase in the
demand for brides with education above primary school. In one
village in which the senior author worked, the wealthiest landowner had arranged to have his daughter marry into a village
well known for its prestige. The agreement was cancelled,
however, when it was found that his daughter did not have a
secondary school education. Since virginity was a requisite for
marriage, it was regarded as unwise to permit a daughter to
leave the village to attend school. It was, therefore, necessary
for the parent to begin a secondary school in his own village in
order that his daughter acquire the necessary educational
certificate. The concern with maintaining the moral reputation
of the girls was also illustrated in Varna village when a woman
teacher was employed to join the staff of male teachers when
the first girls were enrolled. High caste parents were clearly
reluctant to send their post-pubescent daughters to a school of
all male teachers, even though it was in their own village.

Secondary school education was clearly important for boys
for the purpose of qualifying them for a higher occupational level,
but secondary schools were within a few miles of most villages in
the area. A major motive then, for building additional secondary
schools as well as for many already constructed, had to do with

village status and the education of high caste girls to make them more eligible in the marriage market. Given the obvious concern of the village leadership with its secondary school, disinterest on their part in what went on in the school could not be assumed. Any work in the school of an experimental nature had to be approved by the Board. With subjects such as family planning and reproductive education there was good reason to be cautious in approaching village leaders, particularly in view of the concern with maintaining the image of sexual "purity" for their daughters.

At the time of the study, the Varna secondary school had eleven teachers including the one female. Most of the teachers were young. Eight were between 21 and 30 years of age. The curriculum emphasized language study with nine of the eleven teachers instructing part-time or full-time in one or more of four languages: Gujarati, Hindi, English, and Sanskrit. The subjects of next greatest emphasis were mathematics, science and physiology-hygiene with three teachers responsible for these subjects. Geography was taught by two teachers. Another taught social science in addition to English and spelling. Thus, in spite of the language emphasis, there were courses where population material might be integrated into the curriculum.

In order to earn a higher secondary school certificate, it was necessary for a student to pass final examinations in seven subjects. The questions were prepared by the SSC Board and both students and teachers were judged on the basis of the results. All of the students in the study took social studies but only 64 percent of the boys and 58 percent of the girls passed that section of the SSC examination at the end of the school year. Of the 39 students, 31 took the physiology-hygiene course which included "human reproduction". The girls seemingly had more difficulty with the subject since only 45 percent passed, while 75 percent of the boys passed.

All of the teachers in the school were interviewed. Three said they had mentioned in their classes that over-population was a problem for India and there was a need for small families but it was clear that the topic was not emphasized. They generally agreed that such material should be taught in schools but believed that it should be a task for a teacher trained in the area. They did not want to have additional material added to their present teaching load and did not feel prepared to teach it. The teacher

who taught physiology-hygiene reported that although human
reproduction was covered in the text, he did not discuss the text
material in class because he believed it might embarrass the
students. He also expressed concern that if human reproduction,
and particularly family planning, were discussed in the classroom, the relationship between the students and himself would
become too informal. He believed that it would be best to have
a medical person give a talk to the class on such subjects.

Availability of Family Planning Services and Information

Before presenting the content of the students' interviews,
some background on the local family planning program and the
villagers' awareness and acceptance will serve as a reference for
the students' perceptions and responses to questions related to
population problems and family planning.

There were two distinct systems of health services in the
local district. The first consisted of the primary health centers
recently established by the State of Gujarat. The second system
incorporated a series of earlier health units instituted during the
period when this area was part of the princely state of Baroda.
Recent attempts to integrate the two systems had not been
successful because of local politics but both systems were
functioning under a district health officer and a state director of
health and family planning. One of the health units from the
earlier system was located in the village. It was reported to be
serving the local villagers as well as a regional population of
20,000 people. This unit took responsibility for maternal and
child health programs as well as vaccination and tuberculosis
programs, and operated a division of family planning and social
work. The family planning program was added to the health
services in 1965.

Vasectomy operations were performed in the unit's headquarters where IUD's were inserted. Tubectomies, which were
initially an important part of the methods offered by the government program, and more acceptable than vasectomies, had been
greatly restricted because of the cost of patient care and
problems of arranging for hospital facilities in village areas.
Condoms were provided by the family planning unit but were
seldom asked for. The "pill" had not yet been offered.

The local family planning unit had a target of 450 vasectomies and 300 IUD's for 1969; however, from January to July,
only 20 vasectomies had been performed and only seven women
had had the IUD inserted toward these targets. Considerable
efforts had been made in the village and surrounding region to
popularize family planning. Patients who came to the village
clinic were generally advised to practice family planning. Film
shows about family planning, posters, and notices on billboards
all brought family planning messages to the villagers' attention.
A film with a family planning theme had been shown in the central
area of the village several months before the study was carried
out. About 700 villagers (adults and children) had attended.
Models of human reproductive organs and drawings of contraceptives and sterilization operation diagrams were on display in
the unit's headquarters.

In an interview with the health unit's medical officer, he
expressed the feeling that students should be made to understand
the need to limit their family size, and that the school should
teach about family planning. He said he believed that older school
youth already knew about family planning from billboard advertisements, the radio and newspapers, and so there should be no
objection to teaching about family planning in the secondary
school. He thought the Eleventh Standard would be the best point
to introduce "population education" because geography was taught
at this level where it could be incorporated. He also said that he
would be willing to give lectures to the students on "family planning" if he were asked to do so.

The medical officer remarked that the higher caste
villagers were beginning to use the government-approved birth
control methods but that lower caste villagers would not accept
family planning. He said it was difficult to convince the latter to
accept the vasectomy which was available to them free of charge.
He indicated that the unit's social worker and a village level
worker talked to these villagers with little effect on their interest
in having a vasectomy. He believed their behavior was the result
of their lack of education and stubbornness. Then he explained
that some men were so fearful that they would become impotent
after having a vasectomy, that they often refused to come for the
operation after they first agreed and arrangements had been
made. In one instance a medical team had been attacked by villagers to discourage them from offering the vasectomy in that
village.

He explained why the IUD was not popular in the rural
area, saying that it caused bleeding which made women ask to
have the device removed.

In addition to the health unit's family planning program,
the villagers had heard about family planning through the mass
media—the radio, newspapers and movie theaters in the nearby
city. A local radio station carried regular programs and
announcements with family planning messages. With the
increasing availability of Indian-made transistors, almost all the
higher caste families had a radio as well as many lower caste
individuals who had factory jobs in the city. There were over a
dozen movie theaters a few miles away where some of the village
men worked or went for recreation. Women, however, seldom
attended the movie theaters.

There were three Gujarati papers which were delivered to
the village to which many of the higher caste families subscribed,
and papers were also available for customers of local tea stands
which were patronized by village males. News and feature stories
were sometimes read aloud or discussed at the tea stands and
family planning stories and announcements of sterilization camps
were generally to be found in these local papers.

There were then many sources from which village youth
might learn about family planning as well as about the problems
of population growth.

The Students' Responses

As we have seen, the students who make up a village
school in India represent different backgrounds and experiences
just as students do in other communities around the world. Our
objective was to give the reader some feeling for the range of
responses that was given to our questions and the relationship to
home background.

We began by looking at the questions designed to indicate
how aware the students were of population as a problem for India
and for people in their own village. We were also interested in
determining the source of their information about population as
a problem.

Next, and most important, were the possible influences within their own family which may have primary significance in attitude-formation or may have reinforced the information they received from the mass media and other sources.

Following our examination of possible influence patterns, we examined how such influence might be expressed by the students in terms of desired family size and the goals that the students felt may be reached through having large or small families. We then looked at the strength of desire to control the number of children they said they wanted; how many sons and daughters were desired, and how important it was to have a son.

After considering their interests in family planning, we looked at the family action possiblities for effective fertility control. We were interested, for example, in getting some idea of how difficult husband-wife communication might be after marriage and if this would be a possible problem in the adoption of fertility control methods. We also looked at the possible effect of living in the joint family, both in terms of freedom of decision-making on the part of the young couple in terms of desired family size and the control of family size.

We attempted, then, to determine how well informed the students were regarding reproduction and family planning methods. Last, we looked at their responses regarding their feelings about the introduction of population and family planning content into the village school curriculum.

II. Student Awareness of Population Growth
as a National and Village Problem

While we have focused our attention in this monograph on
the possible influence of the family regarding attitudes toward
desired numbers of children and the use of family planning
methods, we also asked more general questions designed to
determine awareness on the part of students of population as a
problem for India and more specifically the village in which the
young people lived.

Problems Faced by the Country

When the students were asked what they thought were some
of the greatest problems faced by the country, economic
responses predominated. Nearly 77 percent commented on the
lack of adequate food, 44 percent mentioned the large number of
poor and 26 percent mentioned unemployment. Shortage of land
and lack of industrialization were commented on by 10 percent
each. The language problem was mentioned by two students,
regional conflict by four, untouchability by three, war by five.
Illiteracy was mentioned by seven students (18 percent).

The interviewers reported that 19 (49 percent) of the
students mentioned population growth of the country as a problem.
When those students who did not mention population were asked if
they thought it was a problem, all agreed that it was. That they
should agree with a question so stated was not surprising. As
pointed out previously, after the first few interviews, it was
evident that some of the students were discussing the interview
questions with their friends so it is likely that most of the class
were soon aware that population and family planning was a major
interest of the interviewers. We must assume that the responses
were influenced by this feedback. As a result, in our analysis
we have given little weight to questions the students could answer
"yes" or "no" to or in a few words. We have paid particular
attention to their explanations of <u>why</u> they felt the way they said
they did. When they were asked <u>why</u> they believed population was
a problem for the country, all of them were able to give one or
more reasons. Comments about food shortages and "starvation"

15

were mentioned by 85 percent, unemployment and job competition by 51 percent, increasing food costs by 16 percent. A few examples will illustrate typical responses.

> High Caste Female (Case 4): You know, Ben [sister], the land does not extend itself, but the population does continue to grow. This leads to a terrible shortage of food. Parents cannot love their children. How can they love all if they have ten or more of them? A mother loses her health if she has many children. People do not get jobs. Parents cannot provide for the education of their children.

> High Caste Male (Case 15): Overpopulation is a problem because whatever success we have with Yojna [family planning or planning], overpopulation continues to increase. As a result, we are not able to progress. Overpopulation also affects our chances for employment. We don't have enough machinery to absorb the entire population. So only a few people are employed. Overpopulation means there is a shortage of food for some persons. Food production has increased in India, but the increase is not sufficient to meet our requirements.

> Scheduled Caste Male (Case 32): Overpopulation is a great problem in India because we do not have enough food to meet the requirements of the large population we have. The result is that we have to import food from the outside. Secondly, unemployment also increases with overpopulation. We have few industries and not many persons are required to work there. As a result of unemployment, there is starvation. When one is not able to earn, how is he going to feed his family? Because of this situation, an employer sometimes takes advantage of us. He pays us less and exploits us.

Village Problems

Although the interviewer had asked specifically about population as a problem in terms of the country in the preceding question, only eight of the 39 students mentioned population when first asked about the problems their own village faced.

While most of the students agreed that it was a problem when specifically asked, most simply agreed without elaboration. What the students talked about were problems of immediate concern rather than possible underlying causes. They talked of inadequate water supply, economic problems, sanitation and drainage difficulties, poor roads and most frequently, the controversy that divided the village at the time—the location of the new school. It should be expected that problems of this kind would be mentioned rather than population growth which may be a contributing cause. What is of concern to those planning programs in population education is how villagers view their problems so that program and curriculum content is relevant to felt needs.

Examples of the comments follow.

High Caste Female (Case 5): Untouchability is a problem because people still isolate them. There is no effort to help the poor and there is no faith in God.

High Caste Female (Case 10): The village has a problem with drinking water. One has to go at midnight to fetch water from the shallow well. The school is not able to accomodate everyone.

High Caste Female (Case 11): The poor in the village have no food to eat. The have no employment. There is also a shortage of housing.

High Caste Male (Case 14): Because the roads are not paved, they are too muddy to use all during the monsoon season.

Population as a Problem

When asked specifically about population as a problem for the village, all but three students said that it was. When the students were asked how population was a problem for the village,

18

Table 3

How Is Population a Problem
for Your Village?

N=36

Response	Number*	Percent
Food shortage	18	50
Unemployment	12	33
School crowding	8	22
Lack of funds for education	4	11
Increasing prices of goods	4	11
Clothing	4	11
Over-crowding on the land or in the village	3	8
Housing-crowding	2	5
Father/mother health	2	5
Inadequate land for cultivation	2	5
Drinking water shortage	2	5
Inadequate medical facilities	2	5
General village progress	1	3
Family conflicts	1	3

*Multiple response

the responses were somewhat different than for general village problems. While such matters as the political difficulties over the new school, the inadequate water supply and sanitation problems were of major concern generally, the students stressed food shortages, unemployment, and inadequate school accomodations as problems aggravated by population growth (Table 3).

A high caste female (Case 8) mentioned the overcrowded living conditions in the village:

The village seems thickly populated. There are so many houses that they seem to be overlapping. This blocks the amount of fresh air one gets and it is not good for the health.

A middle caste youth (Case 36) mentioned the lack of medical services:

There are many sick people but the available doctors
cannot provide the medicine needed by everyone.

But the major concern voiced, particularly by the students
who came from families in economic difficulty, were the
increasing costs and increasing difficulty of obtaining jobs. Of
all costs, the concern over increasing food prices was greatest.

One Scheduled Caste youth (Case 31) saw the food problem
as a recent one:

> Two years ago there was no food shortage in Varna.
> Today there is an acute shortage and what is avail-
> able is sold for a high price.

The relationship between the supply and demand for food
and increasing costs was expressed by a high caste boy (Case
15):

> Overpopulation in the village is a problem because
> we can get food only at high prices. People say
> higher prices are caused by the increase in pop-
> ulation. The requirements of the people increase
> when the size of the family increases. There is
> food shortage so sellers are charging higher prices.

Along with the increase in prices was the more serious
problem of unemployment.

A Scheduled Caste youth (Case 32) pointed to the excess
labor problem:

> As I have said, some of our neighbors and our
> family have little food because of the large size
> of the family and the inadequate earnings of family
> members. The number of people needing work is
> greater than the working people required. This
> is nothing but the effect of overpopulation. This
> is the disadvantage of having a large family.

The problem of lack of work for many in the village was
also expressed by a high caste youth (Case 13):

Overpopulation is a problem in the village because
the amount of land remains the same while the
population increases. Because there are too many
people, some do not get work in the fields. Some
starve when they do not get work. A friend's father
and mother work in the fields but they don't get
jobs. My friend doesn't have food sometimes and
he can't afford school books.

Lack of work was also a problem personally felt by a
lower caste youth (Case 19):

We are unable to get work like we did before.
We used to work as sharecroppers because the
large landowners needed our help. Now it is not
so. I think this is because of the population increase.
There are too many people for the work available.

In two cases, boys from poor families pointed out the
excess of available people for the work to be done; also, one
Scheduled Caste student (Case 29) pointed out that in addition to
the lack of jobs, large landowners could now pay less than they
had in the past:

The Zamindar no longer calls my father to work
the land. He takes those who will work for less.

This was supported by the response of a higher caste youth
(Case 28) who said that his family found no trouble getting the
servants they needed:

Yes, it is a problem. Because people have more
children, the school has had to have longer hours
and has gone to a second shift. Also, unemployment
is increasing. Those who work as laborers get
less money now because there are many who are
willing to work for less. This is evident when
my family employs servants. We find large numbers
of people wanting jobs.

A high caste female student (Case 7) indicated the
discontent that she believed to be occurring and alluded to the
increasing number of jobless and unmet needs and expectations:

Conflict and discontent arise due to scarcity of
resources and people do not get enough to eat.
There are so many people roaming about with
nothing to do.

Conclusion

These 11th Standard students were aware of a wide range
of problems facing their nation. They were able to discuss in
some detail the problems of food shortages and poverty.
Unemployment was stressed particularly by the male students.
In addition to these concerns, a few students mentioned regional
conflicts, language disputes, war with border nations, and
indebtedness to other nations.

Half of the students said overpopulation was a problem in
India but did not elaborate on their response. All of the students,
when asked directly, agreed that population growth was a major
obstacle to national progress. They attributed the food shortages
and the limited amount of land for food production to overpopulation. Unemployment was also viewed as stemming from
rapid population growth.

Population growth was not often given as a major village
problem when the students were first asked to list the most
important problems the village faced. However, when asked
specifically about population as a source of village difficulties,
all but three said it was a problem and were able to give reasons
why it was a concern to the village.

More important, some of the youth, particularly from the
poorer families, related population growth to personal problems
such as unemployment. As we will see, insecurity regarding
getting enough work to supply even basic needs was frequently
expressed.

Government rulings following independence, educational
opportunities and increasing urbanization all were factors in
reducing the dependence of the lower castes and communities on
the large landowners (Zamindar). Traditionally called the jajmani
system, it was a contractual relationship which existed between
the peasant and the landlord. The Zamindar expected life-long

service from the family in a serf-like relationship where family members were almost totally under his control. In return, the contracted family had security and received food and other necessities as well as certain social benefits. While the peasant and his family was freed of this bondage, so was the Zamindar released of responsibility to the family. For many of these families it was difficult to find work other than farm labor and with increasing mechanization and the excess of workers, many of these people seemed to be worse off than under the old system.

Some small landowners were also having difficulty. In addition to the small piece of land of their own, to make enough to live on they would also work the fields of a large landowner. The harvest was usually divided equally. The Agricultural Lands Act of 1947 made such arrangements difficult. The act was designed to give the tenant farmer any land under his cultivation. While some did acquire land, many landowners knew the law was about to be passed and hired day laborers. Others left the land uncultivated. Some even began working the land themselves. Whatever the case, many tenants found themselves without work.

The problems these villagers faced are illustrated in the comments of the lower caste and community boys who complained that the landowners no longer required the service of their families and the boy from the higher caste who said that because of increasing unemployment, his family could hire workers for less money than in the past.

III. Sources of Information about Population
as a Problem for the Nation and the Village

By the time the interviews were conducted, we have seen
that the Indian Government had undertaken an extensive mass
media family planning campaign and the students indicated that it
had been effective in creating awareness.

Newspapers were most frequently mentioned (23 students),
followed by films (13 students), posters (12 students) and radio
(4 students). One student mentioned magazines. In addition to the
mass media, however, there were family planning programs held
in the villages in the area, including film showings, exhibitions
and the visits of family planning workers to the homes. As has
been mentioned, since Varna was a relatively large village, it had
a clinic which disseminated family planning services. These
various family planning activities were also mentioned as a source
of information. The family planning centers (clinics) were
mentioned by seven students, and the visits of the family planning
worker were commented on by eight students.

Eleven students also mentioned friends or relatives as a
source of information. Three students specifically mentioned
discussion with friends while five said that they had either engaged
or listened to general discussion in the village about population
and family planning matters. Two boys said they had talked to
their father about it. Three students reported that a teacher had
discussed it as a problem. A number of students knew that a
census was conducted at regular intervals as a verification of
the fact that the population was growing rapidly and others
commented on the fact that difficulties in the village made it
obvious that there was a population problem.

The comments below illustrate the range of sources of
information mentioned.

High Caste Female (Case 2): The family planning
people make it evident. They have displayed posters.
I also overheard two women talking about overpopulation near the S. T. [State Transport] bus stop.

High Caste Male (Case 26): I learned about the

23

problem of overpopulation and family planning
program after my marriage from the family planning
clinic at Baroda. The clinic taught me about different
family planning devices such as the loop, diaphragm,
cream-jelly applicator and operation.

Lower Caste Male (Case 20): In the village there
is a family planning centre which helps married
couples by giving them contraceptives and performing
operations when requested. Sometimes family
planning camps are set up in the village to insert
loops and perform operations. I have also heard
about overpopulation from seeing family planning
films. A social worker, who had come to see a
neighbor with a large family, also talked about
family planning. He advised an operation. He
said, 'By an operation your family's size will be
controlled and you will be able to take care of your
children nicely. You wouldn't face so many difficulties.' The staff of the family planning centres
are working because of government policy.

Scheduled Caste Male (Case 32): I learned about
the problem of overpopulation and starvation in
India because in the Electricity Board where I
worked, I had many friends who used to talk about
this. I have also seen films about family planning.

Scheduled Caste Male (Case 33): I learned about
the population problem from the newspaper. For
example, I know that every 10 years a census is
taken. From this I have an idea that population
increased rapidly in India. I have learned about
overpopulation from films and the government
family planning program to reduce population.
I have learned about family planning from my
married friend. He has talked to me about such
programs.

While only three students mentioned the teachers as a
source of information, these comments are interesting since they
indicate that at least one teacher did make statements regarding
population and that at least some of the students paid some
attention.

High Caste Female (Case 9): I have heard about
it from elders of the family and a teacher told
us. I have heard it from friends and also read
it in the newspapers.

High Caste Male (Case 13): I consider overpopulation as a problem because our teacher has talked
about it. Our teacher said that more population
affects our employment opportunities. If population
were reduced then probably it would bring good
results in other directions too. Food shortages
would be diminished. These would certainly help
in the progress of India.

Lower Caste Male (Case 17): Overpopulation is
a problem because one day our teacher told us
that due to it we are not able to provide employment
in the village.

Conclusion

The students indicated as sources of information about
population as a problem both mass media and interpersonal
communication. From the standpoint of implications for population education, the frequent reference to the family planning
program may have significance. Many of the students mentioned
the local family planning worker who visited their parents and
neighbors as well as the advertisements and films seen in the
village.

Since there had been no attempt, up to the time of the
study, to include population related matters in the school, the fact
that several students mentioned a teacher as a source was
encouraging. It may also indicate some value of determining what
teachers are already teaching about population related matters
when developing population education programs.

More important perhaps than the school program would be
further development of the family planning program to include
youth. The family planning film shows in the village are attended
by many children and youths. The family planning exhibits also
attract young people. When the family planning worker comes to

visit a home, young people crowd around to hear what she has to say. Since many of these youths will soon be married and since they seem to be getting some information from these activities when focused on adults, family planning workers could be trained to seek them out and answer the questions of younger people.

While the students interviewed were all in school, most youths their age are not. For all age groups in India at the secondary level (14-17) for 1973, 30 percent of males and only 12 percent of females were enrolled (Nortman and Hofstatter, 1975). School programs then are likely to reach few boys and even fewer girls and those who are reached are likely to come from high caste and educated families where knowledge of family planning is most adequate. The need for out-of-school programs for youth is obvious and for this region at least, current government activities suggest what might be done for little additional cost.

IV. Parental Expression Regarding Family Size
Preference and Family Size Limitation

We have seen that most of the students seem to have
learned that population growth was a problem for the country, and
at a more meaningful level, for the village. Next we will examine
more closely the kind of learning experiences within their own
families which may have influenced attitude formation regarding
personal family size preferences and family size limitation.

We asked the students what they thought were some
of the problems in their own family. We then asked about the
kinds of problems that were discussed in the home and if their
parents talked about the size of the family as one of the problems.

We have reported that the students differed in their backgrounds in terms of social status and family income, as well as
family size. Obviously these variables were important in
determining their responses to our questions. In order to
organize the students into groups for further analysis, we first
used the responses to the question about general family problems.

The students could be divided into two major groups, those
from high caste families and those from lower castes and low
status communities. However, it was obvious that not all high
caste families had similar incomes and standards of living. In
addition to varying degrees of economic difficulties, there was a
wide range of differences in other problems. We therefore
divided the students from high caste families into three groups:
those who said there were no major family problems, those who
stated there were problems but not primarily economic ones, and
a third group whose major complaints had to do with economic
concerns. The lower caste group and those from scheduled
castes and tribes were all low income families with economic
problems.

In the interviews it was obvious that some of the boys and
girls were only guessing, while others seemed more certain about
the sources and amount of family income. Our feeling was that
those from the most well-to-do famllies were likely to be the
least accurate, because family income was not as important in

27

their lives as it was to students in poorer families and less likely
to be discussed. Because we were unsure of the responses in
this subject area, we have generally not reported income for
specific families. However, the average income we have reported
for the sample divisions is probably close to typical incomes for
families in those socio-economic brackets. We reported that the
family of a wealthy landowner may have had an annual income as
high as Rs. 16,000 while the poorest families of day laborers
seemed to be closer to Rs. 500 a year. Students from high caste
families with no economic problems reported an average annual
income of Rs. 6,500 while those from high caste families with
economic problems reported annual incomes of Rs. 2,600. The
lower caste families averaged Rs. 1,325 while the income for
scheduled caste and tribe families was Rs. 563 (Table 4). This
wide range of income by caste and communities is supported by
Anker (1973) who conducted an intensive investigation of the
economic status of a sample of 467 families in eleven villages in
the same area as Varna village.

In the student data the average number of children in the
families who had to share the available income was large for
all groups but it generally increased as income became lower.
Those families with the highest average incomes had 4.4 children
on the average while those with the lower incomes had 5.0
children (Table 4).

In the high castes, the difference between the group with
no stated problems and those with problems had to do with the
larger number of girls in the second group and the larger number
of reported deaths of children. In some of these families, it was
obvious that having too many daughters had caused problems,
particularly in regard to marriage arrangements. While it was
clear that there was an underreporting of infants' and children's
deaths, particularly of daughters, the generally higher educational
level of the fathers in the higher income group, as well as the
financial ability to provide medical care, probably resulted in
lower infant and child mortality.

Some explanation is needed for the fact that in almost all
families, in all groups, and in the families of the girls as well
as the families of the boys, there were fewer living girls than
boys. For the total group there was an average of 4.7 children
in the families of the students, with 2.8 sons and 1.9 daughters.

Table 4

Average Number of Living Children, and Number Who Died, and
Yearly Family Income for Families of Higher and Lower Caste Communities

	Higher Castes			Lower Castes	Scheduled Castes & Tribes
	No problems N=6	Non-economic problems N=7	Economic problems N=14	N=4	N=8
Average children living					
Boys	3.2	2.6	2.6	3.0	3.0
Girls	1.2	1.7	2.2	1.5	2.0
Total	4.4	4.3	4.8	4.5	5.0
Average children died					
Boys	0	.3	.4	.3	.5
Girls	0	.1	.7	.5	.4
Total	0	.4	1.1	.8	.9
Total born	4.4	4.7	5.9	5.3	5.9
Average Income	Rs. 6,830	Rs. 6,163	Rs. 2,608	Rs. 1,325	Rs. 563

Female infanticide has not been an uncommon practice in
Gujarat in the past, particularly in the higher castes where large
dowries have been a significant drain on joint family resources
(Mehta, 1966). When asked what ways they knew to keep from
having a baby, one of the girls said:

> The operation and the loop are ways to keep from
> having children. I do not know much about it, but
> I know if there is an unwanted child born and if it
> is a girl, it is taken some place and is gotten rid
> of.

This was the only remark of the kind and the villagers
would not discuss the subject. It has been our feeling in the past
that the sex imbalance has been due to neglect which often results
in the death of a daughter within the first year or so of life.
However, it is possible that outright infanticide was still practised
on occasion.

Once we divided our cases by economic and social status,
we did a content analysis of the series of questions designed to
determine parental communication regarding desired family size
and attitudes toward family limitation. The responses seemed to
fall into five groupings of parental expression: expressed need
for control of family size; expressed need for others to control
family size; no parental discussion but apparent communication of
the need for control of family size; no parental discussion of
family size; expressed preference for a large family (Table 5).

We will first present a brief picture of each of the families
by economic and caste and community groupings in terms of the
difficulties that were reported and what indications were given of
possible parental attitudes regarding family size and family
limitation. We will then attempt to summarize the findings.

High Caste Family Has No Problems

Of the 39 students, six reported that there were no
serious problems in their family. All of these students were
from high caste families with incomes far beyond the average for
the area under study.

Table 5. Case Number and Number of Living Sons (S) and Daughters (D) by Assessment of Parental Expression Regarding Family Size Limitation from Student Comments and Socio-Economic and Status Groupings

Parental Expression	High Caste									Lower Caste			Scheduled Castes and Tribes			Total Cases	
	No Problems			Non-economic Problems			Economic Problems										
	Case	S	D	Case	S	D	Case	S	D	Case	S	D	Case	S	D	N	%
Expressed need for control of family size	27	2	3	26	5	0	3*	2	2	17	2	3	29	4	2	12	31
							14	2	1	20	5	3	31	2	2		
							15	4	2				32	3	2		
							38	1	2				33	2	2		
Expressed need for others to control family size	13	3	1													3	8
	22	4	1														
	37	3	0														
No parental discussion but apparent communication of the need for control of family size				7	2	2	10	3	3	19	3	1	30	4	1	9	23
				8	1	2							34	3	2		
				25	3	3							35	3	2		
													36	4	3		
Parental ambivalence regarding control of family size							1	1	2								
							4	1	3								
							5	4	2								
							9	5	3								
							11	3	2								
							12	5	2								
No parental discussion of family size	16	3	1				23	2	3	18	2	2				3	8
Expressed preference for a large family	24	4	1	6	4	1	2	0	3							6	15
				28	3	3	21	4	1								
				39	0	1											

*Female cases are underlined.

Expressed preference for a large family. Although these students
were under little economic strain, in only one case was it
indicated that a big family was preferred to a small one by the
parents.

High Caste Male (Case 24). There were five living
children in the family, four sons (ages 8, 11, 15, and 17), and one
daughter (age 9). The children were all attending school. The
father was a merchant living in East Africa where the boy was
born. His uncle and grandmother lived with the mother and
children. The boy said that family problems were not discussed
and as far as he was concerned there were no major problems.
He said that his mother liked many children. He seldom saw his
father and was not sure of what his father believed.

> My mother likes a big family. She would prefer
> to have children in the house even if it were ex-
> pensive to have so many. I am not certain what
> my father thinks about family size. He probably
> does not mind having a large family if the sons
> could obtain good jobs and contribute part of their
> income to the family.
>
> If we had a small family, my mother would have
> great fear that some of her children would die and
> she would be afraid that no one would live to keep
> her company.

No parental discussion of family size. Of this group, one boy was
unaware of discussions about family size on the part of his
parents. However, he said that he had learned about the problem
from his friends.

High Caste Male (Case 16). There were four living
children in the family, three sons (ages 9, 10, and 17) and one
daughter (age 8). The children were all attending school. The
father was a landowner with a cash income from farming. The
boy felt that the family income was adequate for the family.

> My father and mother talk about adjusting our
> needs to our income but they do not discuss the
> size of the family.

I have learned about family size problems from
my friends. They regard their family size as a
problem because of their poor financial condition.
They cannot go on for higher education because
their families have many children and little income.

Expressed need for others to control family size. In three others
of these well-to-do families, the students reported that their
parents did talk about family size, not in terms of their own
family, but in terms of others.

High Caste Male (Case 13). There were four living
children in the family, three sons (ages 14, 16, and 24), and one
daughter (age 20). The older brother was married and lived in the
city with his family. He was employed as an inspector in a
factory. The daughter was also married, living in another
village. The younger boy was in school. The father was a landowner. He said that his mother and father discussed family
planning but the interview material did not indicate specific
references to their own extended family.

My mother and father talk about the advantages
of having a small family when they are with neighbors
or friends. I have heard them say, 'It is enough
to have one son only, then insert a loop.'

High Caste Male (Case 22). There were five living
children in the family, four sons (ages 7, 8, 18, and 22), and one
daughter (age 15). They were all attending school. The father
was a medical practitioner. He said his father had an adequate
income and the family members got along well together. His
awareness of family size limitation resulted in part from hearing
his father and mother talk with patients.

My father believes in family planning. If his patients
have more children than they can afford, he talks
to them about it. My mother also talks to the women
if they have large families. She says, 'Why don't
you go to the Family Planning Centre?'

High Caste Male (Case 37). There were three living
children in the family, all sons (ages 17, 22, and 28). The father
was a landowner. In addition, the oldest son had a steady income

34

as a teacher. The middle brother was a college student. The boy
reported no serious family planning problems although he said his
parents did discuss the increasing cost of living.

> Yes, my father and mother talk about a small
> family. When they see a large family suffering
> from any difficulties, they talk about the benefits
> of a small family.

<u>Expressed need for control of family size</u>. In the case of one of
the six students in the group, in addition to recommending a
small family for others, the parents had told the boy he should
limit his own family size.

> High Caste Male (Case 27). There were five children in
the family, two sons (ages 17 and 25), and three daughters (ages
6, 10, and 12). The father was a landowner. In addition, the
oldest son worked in a factory in the city. The rest of the
children were in school.

> We live contentedly and rarely quarrel about any-
> thing. We have a good income and there is good
> cooperation among family members.

> My father has told me to have a small family.
> He once showed me a poster about family planning,
> saying that in order to make both my life and the
> lives of my children happy that I should have a
> small family.

> My mother agrees with my father that a small
> family is best. She once talked to a servant of
> ours who had seven children and was not well.
> She told her she should see a doctor and take care
> of herself. She recommended to the servant that
> she get herself sterilized.

> There are no advantages to having a large family.
> You cannot do the things which are necessary for
> the future of your children if you have too many.
> Our neighbors have a small income and a large
> family and although the father wants his sons to
> become educated, he is finding it difficult to provide
> for their education.

High Caste Family Has Non-economic Problems

There were seven high caste families where the students reported problems but said they were not economic in nature. However, many of the problems did seem to relate to economic factors. Illness, in spite of improved health services, continued to be a major problem and some of the concern about it was because of its potential in depriving the family of significant contributing members. Concern with the lack of presence or the behavior of a son was also stated. Here again the reason behind the concern was the fear that a son would not meet family needs and these were usually stated in economic terms. Other problems centered around family conflicts but these were often over money or land.

Expressed preference for a large family. Of the seven students in this group, three regarded their parents as wanting a large family with no indication of a desire to control fertility. The major theme in each case seemed to be concern about a son taking over family responsibility.

High Caste Female (Case 6). There were five children in the family, four sons (ages 6, 10, 13, and 18), and one daughter (age 17). The daughter (student) had recently married but had not yet gone to live with her in-laws. She said her father was a landowner and that he and his eldest sons worked the land. Their greatest problem seemed to be illness in the family and a shortage of space in the home for the family members.

> My father would agree with my mother, that a
> large family is desirable. So family size is not
> a big question for us. Only when my father is
> tired after work, he sometimes feels that now
> my oldest brother should take over the responsi-
> bility for the younger ones. When he is tired he
> thinks there are too many children around.

High Caste Male (Case 28). There were six children in the family, three sons (ages 17, 24, and 30), and three daughters (ages 23, 24, and 28). All the daughters were married and living with their husbands. The older brothers were also married and lived in the city with their families. The father was a farmer-landowner.

The eldest brother was a mill worker with an income of Rs. 270 a month, but he had a family of four children to care for. The middle brother also worked in the mill. Although the father had a good income from the farm, he was getting older and concerned that his sons might not support him after he could no longer work. Both the mother and father were regarded by the student as preferring a large family.

> There is no family problem, except with my uncle regarding the family property. My brothers stay in the city and my sisters are married. So there are only four of us here. My mother does not allow me to play the radio because my father has constant stomach aches. When my second brother failed his SSC my father became very angry. He wanted him to study further so he could get a good job. He is concerned about who will care for him when he is old. My oldest brother has a big family and because of this my father fears he may shirk his duty of caring for my father.

> My mother and father like a large family. If the family were too small, my mother would have more household duties to perform. My father would not have the monetary contributions of his sons.

High Caste Female (Case 39). The effect of the lack of a son was evident in this family. There was only one child in the family (the student, age 18). She lived alone with her mother since the father had committed suicide when the girl was a year old. The mother had suffered considerable emotional stress over the years since the father's family continued to create problems for her. The mother and daughter recently moved to Varna village where the mother was teaching school. Her income was Rs. 164 per month.

> We are lonely because of my father's death. On top of it, we have to face the court to prove that he is actually dead. His sister claims that my father is still living someplace and that my mother should consent to a divorce. How can one divorce a person who is no longer living? Whatever property

we had has been taken over by my aunt. My mother
is in bad health with stomach aches. She cannot
eat or work hard. I have to do much of the work
for her. Another problem is that I was to marry
but it has been broken off. Perhaps my aunt also
played a role in this.

Money is not a problem because of my mother's
brother. He is an angel and helps us a lot.

My mother feels it would have been better if she
could have had a son. But maybe she feels a
daughter-in-law would not be as loyal to her as
her own daughter is.

My mother has the same ideas as I do. She thinks
a large family provides an opportunity for the
children to learn to assume responsibilities.
This frees the parents. There are economic
advantages to a large family also.

No parental discussion but apparent communication of the need
for control of family size. The fear that his death would leave
younger children vulnerable seemed to be a factor in terminating
fertility in one of the three families in this group. Concern with
the illness of grandchildren seemed indicated on the part of
another father. For one boy the crowding of members of a large
family seemed to have influenced his feelings about family size.

High Caste Female (Case 7). There were four children
in the family, two sons (ages 10 and 18), and two daughters (ages
8 and 16). The father was a landowner and farmed with the help
of the oldest son. The student did not mention economic problems
but said family members were concerned about the illness of her
father. Family size was not discussed directly. However, the
girl was aware that her parents were sufficiently concerned about
preventing another pregnancy for the mother to have a tubectomy.

We do not have many problems in our family, except
that my father is tired of his sickness. He worries
about what would happen to my younger brother if
he died. Who would educate him? Because of
his illness, I think there has been a kind of worry

about the younger children. Now my mother has
been operated on for family planning purposes.

High Caste Female (Case 8). In this extended family there
were three children, one son (age 25) and two daughters (ages 17
and 32). The son was married and he and his wife with their
three children lived with the family. The older daughter lost her
husband and was also living with the family along with her three
children. The father was a landowner.

The brother had a job in the city. The family did not seem
to have major economic problems, but the girl complained of
family members' illness and the costs of treatment. With six
small children in the family there was much illness. This
seemed to be the major topic discussed, but she did feel her
father and mother would prefer a small family.

The main problems they discuss when I am around
are sickness in the family and a shortage of food
grains. Sickness is our permanent guest. The
whole family is sick. God knows why! No specific
remarks are made about this, but it is generally
understood in my family that my father feels that
the doctor's bills would be smaller if we were a
smaller family.

The money spend on food and clothing would be less
in a small family. It is easier to move around.
There are fewer conflicts in a small family because
you can get what is necessary. A mother would
have fewer worries and would be able to preserve
her health.

My father would also favor a small family. There
would be fewer worries about illness as there would
be fewer members in the family. There would
be no conflicts. A father could satisfy his children's
demands for toys.

High Caste Male (Case 25). There were six children in
the family, three sons (ages 17, 30, and 40), and three daughters
(ages 20, 22, and 35). The daughters were married so the costs
and problems of such arrangements were past for the parents.

The two older brothers were also married and lived in the
extended family with their wives and children. The father was a
cloth merchant and the brothers worked with him.

The only problem the student reported was the lack of
space for all the family members. He did not know what his
mother and father thought about family size since he said it was
never discussed. Even so, the boy seemed to have his own
opinion, seemingly from observing his brother's children
around the house.

> My father and mother never talk about family size.
> Since we live in the joint family, there is little
> chance for my parents to discuss things like that,
> but if our family size had been smaller, we would
> have had more space. Space is our problem.

> I, myself, see no advantages in having a large
> family. Too many small children are had to control
> and cause confusion in the family. It is impossible
> for parents to pay enough attention to their needs
> and to their education. This is especially true
> if the husband's income is limited. I also believe
> that too many pregnancies can hurt a mother's
> health and this affects the health of the babies
> as well.

Expressed need for control of family size. In the one high caste
family in this group, extended family quarrels about land seemed
to have been a factor in parental advice to the student to limit
his family size.

High Caste Male (Case 26). There were five children in
the family, all of them boys (ages 11, 14, 17, 20, and 22). The
two eldest brothers were married. The father was a landowner.
The student had recently been married but his bride had not yet
come to live with him and the joint family. He did not comment
on economic problems but talked of the quarrels that took place
in a large joint family. In this case, not only had family planning
been discussed, but the boy's mother had told him and his bride
that they should have a small family.

> We have a problem over land which was left to
> the family. An uncle also claims the land and

there is a court case over it. A large family makes
for quarrels over ownership of family property.
Quarrels often take place.

From my parents' talk it comes out that they do
not like a large family. They talk about family
planning but not openly to everyone. My mother
advised my wife to have a small family when she
was here the first time. I was not present but she
talked to me separately.

High Caste Family Has Economic Problems

Being a member of a high caste family did not mean
economic security. More than half of the students from high
caste families specifically referred to family problems of an
economic nature. The economic problems seemed to center
around sons; the lack of sons, their education, the inadequate
nature of the income they received or the fact that one or more
sons had no job at all. Concerns about sons also seemed to be
associated with a desire for a large family or parental ambivalence about family size and family size control.

Expressed preference for a large family. The anxiety felt by a
woman who had no living son was evident in one case where more
children were desired. In another case, in spite of the economic
stress of educating five sons, the parents gave no indication of
change from a large family orientation.

High Caste Female (Case 2). There were three children
in the family, all daughters (ages 17, 20, and 22). The father
was a landowner. The lack of a son in the family was a major
concern.

My mother has not been in good health. She has
high blood pressure and her hands get numb.
Our income is not adequate and we do not have
a good house. I do not have a brother. We should
have a son in the house. I think I will have to
shoulder the responsibility of the family and look
after everything.

The size of the family is not discussed except
that my mother would like to have a bigger family
to have a son. My father would like a son to look
after him in old age and my mother would like a
daughter-in-law to come when her daughters have
left the home. There is a belief that a son can
perform the final rites and pave the parents' way
to heaven. I would not believe in this heaven business,
but a son is essential to the family in other ways.
I would also wish to be supported and be looked
after by my children in my old age.

High Caste Male (Case 21). There were five children in
the family, four sons (ages 15, 16, 17, and 23), and one daughter
(age 25). The daughter and her two children lived with the family.
The father was also a village leader, and as with other high status
Patidar farmers, the cost of higher education for many sons
resulted in feelings of economic stress. The student reported that
family problems were discussed but not family size. However, he
felt that neither of his parents would favor a small family.

The biggest problem of the family is money. My
elder brother is in the Commerce College. His
education is expensive. My father is afraid that
all of us might ask for a university education.
How would he manage? He would have to borrow
and we would have to pay interest on the debt.
The rising cost of living is also discussed. Family
size is not talked about. . . at least I do not know
of it.

I do know my father would not feel good about having
a small family. The disadvantage he might point
out is only having daughters. When they would
go away after marriage, there would be nothing
left.

My mother would never think of a small family.
A large family has many advantages. She would
feel that in the case of a mishap such as the death
of children, we would have others to grow up.

No parental discussion of family size. In one case in this group, money was stated as a problem only in terms of the need for marriage arrangements of daughters and education for sons, and family size did not seem to be a parental concern.

High Caste Male (Case 23). There were five children in the family, two sons (ages 17 and 21), and three daughters (ages 9, 12, and 14). The father was a landowner. The oldest brother was attending college in the city and the father planned to send the younger son through college. With the cost of education and the added cost of marriage for the maturing daughters, money was of concern to the family. However, he said that family size was not specifically discussed and he did not know what his parents thought about it.

> The only problem we have is arranging the marriage
> of my sister. We must obtain money for a dowry.
> However, I think we can cope with the problem
> by earning more money. We also have some savings.

> My father talks about my education and the marriage
> of my sisters. Family size is not a problem and
> I have never heard it discussed or family planning
> discussed. I have no idea what my parents think
> about family size.

Parental ambivalence regarding control of family size. The most frequent expression of ambivalence regarding family size was found in this group of high caste families where the students said there were economic problems. A common theme seemed to center around the need for sons for economic help, but there was concern that once the investment in rearing and education was made, a son might leave the family, would not be able to make enough money to help or would be unable to get a job at all.

High Caste Female (Case 1). There were three children in the family, one son (age 13), and two daughters (ages 17 and 20). The older sister was married and living with her in-laws. The children lived with their father and his older brother. The mother had died some years before.

The father and brother were landowners. The father's major concern was raising the money for a dowry for his younger daughter's marriage. She was not sure what her father's feelings were about family size, but knew that he would like to have had an older son.

> My mother's death was a problem for us. She
> died almost ten years ago. I was seven and my
> sister was two years old. My mother died of
> cancer. My father worries a lot. He must arrange
> my marriage. Money is a problem because my
> family cannot afford the costs of a marriage for
> me. I have one sister who is married which cost
> a lot.

> My father and uncle talk a lot about money. I
> think that father would prefer a small family, but
> he would feel that a son is necessary. If he had
> had a son early in marriage, the son could be
> helping him now, and the son's wife could be looking
> after the home. I would agree with this. A son
> would help take care of him in his old age. But
> I don't know about girls. They have to be married,
> and a dowry is always necessary. Still, a girl
> is useful. She can work and be helpful to the
> household.

High Caste Female (Case 4). There were four children in the family, three daughters (ages 12, 14, and 17), and one son (age 23). An older sister died giving birth and the mother had the care of the daughter's child. The girl said the death of her sister was a great shock to their mother.

The father was a Brahmin priest who had been forced to take a low status job as a postman because he lost the right to the income from the temple land. The family problems were compounded by the fact that the only son left the family and was not making an economic contribution. Family size seemed to have been discussed only in terms of the fact that the parents had only one son and that he had not played his expected traditional role.

> My family has many problems. My mother is in
> bad health. I don't know exactly how old my parents
> are. I am surprised at how old my mother looks.
> She must be younger than my father but she has

gray hair and looks completely worn out. My
sister died leaving a child behind for my mother
to care for. Also, my older brother has left our
family. We have to buy food grains and we have
no land for income. We used to have land that
was given to my forefathers who came here as
temple priests. My father worked that land and
served the temple and we were able to maintain
ourselves. Then my father gave the land to my
brother but the villagers opposed this and took
the land. Now my brother has separated from
the family and the income from the temple is not
enough. The house which was already too small
for us has been divided for more income, so we
have little space. I know my father is worried
about the children. He tries to deal with the
problems. He has taken a job as a postman in
the village. My brother's attitude is openly criticized
by my parents. Since he will not live with us anymore,
who will look after the family when my father gets
old or dies?

Both my father and mother have wished for sons
and the one son they had left the family. This
has caused them great distress.

High Caste Female (Case 5). There were six children in
the family, four boys (ages 8, 12, 14, and 18) and two girls (ages
16 and 22). The oldest girl was married. The rest were
students. The father was a merchant. The father lost money in
the transaction of property and extended family members blamed
him for it. The oldest brother was no longer going to school and
had not yet found employment so this was a source of concern to
the father. A marriage had been arranged for the respondent.
The student had heard her parents discuss their family size and
indicated there may have been disagreement betweeen the mother
and father regarding desired numbers of children.

My parents talk about how big our family is and
how difficult it is to maintain. I do not know much
about it but I feel my father worries about all the
children. But my father likes a big family. If
there were more sons in the family, then there

would be more income to be pooled. If there was
a small family and the children died at a young
age, the parents would be lonely. My mother may
not agree with my father's views, but she would
have to follow him.

I think if there is adequate income, there is
nothing like the fun of a big family.

High Caste Female (Case 9). There were eight children
in the family, five sons (ages 12, 17, 19, 21, and 35), and three
daughters (ages 16, 30, and 40). The father died several years
before the interview. All of the children were married except the
respondent and her youngest brother. The eldest brother farmed
a small piece of land owned by the family while the next two sons
had been forced to take poor paying jobs in a town over 50 miles
from the village. Since the father died, the eldest brother had
had full responsibility for the farm and the girl reported that the
annual yield had dropped.

At the time of the interview, even the combined income of
all three brothers seemed to be inadequate to meet minimal family
needs. The girl said her mother felt the strain of a big family
under the present circumstances but that she would enjoy it if the
income were adequate.

My father died so we have an economic problem.
We cannot even purchase food grains on a yearly
basis and we have gone into debt. My uncle has
had to help us.

My mother is concerned about the family size.
She does say that if there had been fewer children
there might have been fewer worries for her.
The cost of education, marriage and maintenance
would have been smaller. However, my mother
feels that once her sons get settled and earning
well, there will be nothing like her big family.

High Caste Female (Case 11). There were five children in
the family, three sons (ages 11, 14, and 18), and two daughters
(ages 16 and 17). The father was a landowner.

The cost of arranging marriages for the two daughters and educating the sons was of major concern. Economic problems were discussed but the girl reported no discussion of family size. Still, she had some idea about how her parents felt about family size. She felt her mother would have had fewer children but that her father had wanted a large family.

My parents do talk about their problems... such a
as money and their debt, but the size of the family
is not discussed in our presence. I do not know
if they talk about it or not.

I think my father would not appreciate a small
family, but my mother would prefer fewer children.
She feels a small family is less bothersome.
But still to her a son is a must. A son is a gift
from God who works for the family. You spend
on him today and he pays dividends by looking
after the family later. Girls are married away
and give no support. Our belief does not permit
a family to maintain itself on the income of a
daughter. To do so would be regarded as a sin.

High Caste Female (Case 12). In this large joint family, there were seven children, five brothers (ages 9, 12, 20, 23, and 26) and two sisters (ages 8 and 16). The older brother was married and lived with his wife in the family home. The father's sisters also lived with the family. The father was a medical practitioner.

The eldest son also had had some medical training and worked as a vaccinator. In spite of the combined income of the father and brother, the girl said there was never enough money to meet the family's needs. The father's sister was not able to adjust to the family of her in-laws so had been sent back to her family. Two of the brothers had been unable to find employment. The problem of family size was discussed in the home. The advantages of a small family were recognized but so were the advantages of a large family. However, the mother had had a tubectomy several years previously.

They [parents] talk about the size of our family.
I may not be expected to participate, but my

presence is not objected to. They talk about the
problems of scarcity of money and the unemployment
of my brothers. They do talk about the size of
our family and my mother has had an operation
to stop having children.

We try our best to cope with our difficulties.
My brothers keep searching for jobs. My father
still continues to negotiate with our in-laws for
'Auntie'.

My father thinks a small family presents fewer
problems. He would have fewer worries about
providing clothing and arranging marriages. My
mother also feels there would be fewer problems
finding mates for her daughters but also wonders
if one or two children were lost, how could she
live.

The fun of living together is one thing good about
a large family. We are all fond of singing together.
We hardly feel like going out because we are such
a good group. One also gets help in the household
routines in a large family.

<u>No parental discussion but apparent communication of the need</u>
<u>for control of family size</u>. In one case with the increasing needs
of six growing children all dependent on the father, the student
said that although the size of the family was not discussed
directly, other problems were discussed which related to
problems of family size.

High Caste Female (Case 10). There were six children
in the family, three sons (ages 5, 13, and 15), and three
daughters (ages 6, 16, and 18). The father was a landowner.
All of the children were in school. The youngest brother had
polio and was a major family concern. The girl indicated that
her parents were also very concerned about the problems and
costs of arranging marriages for herself and her younger sister.

Yes, problems are discussed when I am present.
My father and mother talk about the problem of
maintaining the family. Ours is a big family and

our income is not sufficient. This creates tension
in my family.

I think my mother would like a small family, but
I don't know what my father's views are.

Expressed need for control of family size. In four cases, there
was direct expression on the part of the parents regarding the
need to control family size   The factors expressed as important
in parental attitude had to do with inadequate income, need for
more housing, marriage costs and, in one case, the fact that the
mother had almost died during the birth of her last child.

High Caste Female (Case 3). There were four children in
the family, two sons (ages 6 and 15), and two daughters (ages 9
and 17). The father farmed a small piece of land. The
respondent said her parents would prefer a small family and that
her mother had had a tubectomy.

Our family has many problems. We do not have
a [dairy] buffalo. Our farm is not adequate.
There is not enough money. We cannot feed the
oxen properly and we are in debt.

My parents like a small family, but my father would
want a son to care for him and I would like one
also. A daughter is a liability. My mother feels
that girls are someone else's property because
they have to be given away when they are grown
up.

My parents have used family planning. My mother
first had a loop inserted, but it did not suit her.
Now she has had an operation.

High Caste Male (Case 14). There were three children,
two sons (ages 16 and 18), and one daughter (age 12). All were
unmarried. The father was a landowner. The older brother
worked the farm with his father. The boy complained of living in
an old house in need of repair. He said his parents preferred a
small family and he had discussed this with his friends.

The main problem my father talks about with my

mother is house-building. We need to expand our
house.

My father and mother do have a certain taste for
a small family which may be seen in our own small
family. They believe that in spite of our small
income, we live happily due to the number of children
in our home.

My friends also think a small family is best. I
have already told you that the land remains the
same while the family size becomes larger and
larger. This will continue to happen if we do not
control the size of our families after we are married.

High Caste Male (Case 15). The family had six children,
four sons (ages 15, 17, 20, and 23), and two daughters (ages 8
and 18). The older brother was married and lived in the joint
family with his wife and one child. The father was a landowner.
The oldest son was employed in the city. However, the family
was in debt because of social obligations which were
characteristic of high Patidar families. The parents felt the
family was too large and had told the boy to limit the size of his
own family.

My family is in debt because of my sister's dowry.
My father borrowed on his land to pay it. We earn
enough money for common needs but things like
marriage, a naming ceremony or a pregnancy
ceremony make us borrow. If we did not have
these expenses we could save some of our income.
Instead, just now my father is trying to sell another
part of our land.

My mother and father do talk about our debt and
family size. They believe a smaller family would
have fewer problems. Also with a smaller family,
quarrels could be avoided when it came time to
divide the land among brothers. Land is a problem.
Some of my friends have large families and they
have divided even a small amount of land. Now it
is impossible for them to make a living on it.

Because of these problems, I have often heard
my parents say to us that we should keep our
families small or we will be in the same position.

High Caste Male (Case 38). There were three living
children in this family, two girls (ages 13 and 19) and the
respondent, a boy (age 16). None of the children were married.
The father was no longer living. With the father dead, there was
no male earning member of the family. The mother had a small
pension of Rs. 500 a year and the children farmed their small
piece of land.

The mother almost died several years before at the time of
a stillbirth of twins. She had never fully recovered from the
experience. Family planning problems were discussed within the
family and the mother was in favor of sterilization.

Our biggest problem is economic because there
is no full-time earning member. But we are only
three children and that is a small family. My
mother does talk to our neighbors about it. She
says that many deliveries are not good because
they affect the health of the woman as well as the
child. She thinks that after two or three children,
one should have a sterilization. I fully agree with
this view because I saw what my mother's condition
was after the birth of the twins.

Lower Castes

Of the four lower caste families, one student reported no
economic problems. The other three had economic difficulties.

No parental discussion of family size. It was the student who
reported no economic problems in the home who also said there
was no discussion of family size. The income was similar to that
of poorer high caste families but since there were lower social
expectations and only four children, the income seemed to be
adequate.

Lower Caste Male (Case 18). There were four children in

the family, two sons (ages 16 and 18), and two daughters (ages 13 and 15). The father owned enough land for him and the older brother to bring in about Rs. 2,000 a year from cash crops. With a relatively good income and four children, the father was concerned about social status and arranging a "good" marriage for his eldest daughter. Family size was not discussed in the home, but it was with his friends.

> We have no problem except with my sister's
> marriage. My father always thinks about it.
> My parents worry about finding a suitable mate
> for her.

> I have never heard my mother and father talking
> about the size of the family we have. They talk
> about marriage problems and education. So I do
> not know what my parents think about it. My friends
> talk about it because they are very poor and are
> members of large families.

<u>No parental discussion but apparent communication of the need for control of family size.</u> In one case there was family discussion about economic problems but not about family size. However, he knew that his stepmother had accepted an IUD and that his father was concerned about how he would be able to give each of his children the education he believed was necessary.

Lower Caste Male (Case 19). There were four children in the family, the student (age 19), and the three younger children of his stepmother. The student's mother died when he was ten years old and he had no living brothers or sisters. The father remarried and the stepmother and her three children were living with the family. The father worked his own small piece of land, and on weekends he farmed for a large landowner. The student helped him on the farm after school.

> Our main problem is money. We have only Rs. 600
> a year income and the whole family depends on this.
> My stepmother also quarrels a lot about who is to
> do the work.

> We never talk much about the problem of too many

children in the home. For the most part because
we are all very active and haven't time for discussing
such things. I work for two or three hours in the
morning in the fields, then I have to go to school.
After school I work in the fields again. After dark
it is time for me to do my lessons. So I am very
busy and have little opportunity to talk with anyone.

I know my father is concerned about my future
and wants my children to have even more education
than is planned for me. It would have been better
for our family if there had only been two children.
Then we would have more money to spend. But
now my stepmother has had a loop inserted so there
will be no more children.

Expressed need for control of family size. Of the two students
who indicated parental expression of a need to control family size,
one had brothers and sisters at the ages of greatest cost in terms
of education and marriage. In the second family, the discussion
on the part of the father had to do with the eldest son whom he
felt had too many children, leaving no income to contribute to the
joint family.

Lower Caste Male (Case 17). There were five children in
the family, two sons (ages 12 and 16), and three daughters (ages
7, 10, and 14). The father was a small landowner. The boy saw
life as a constant economic crisis because of the family debt.
Both economic problems and the family size were discussed.

We have a large family and our income is very
small. We try to cope with the problem by working
two crops a year.

My father and mother do sit together and discuss
the problems of our family size. They talk of the
costs of education, religious festivals and other
things that must be celebrated.

My father believes small families are good. When
we have to borrow money he always says a small
family would have been better. When my mother
goes to the shop to buy supplies she has told me,

"We must buy food from the shops but we earn
very little. If there are more children, more must
be earned. It is best to earn more but to keep
the family size down. This will bring happiness."

Lower Caste Male (Case 20). There were five children
in the family, all sons (ages 16, 18, 20, 25, and 27). The father
served as a clerk in the city. The mother did part-time tailoring
in the home, the traditional occupation of the caste. The two
older sons had left the family and were working as tailors in the
city. The third brother was recently employed as a clerk in a
nursing home and continued to live in the village. In spite of the
economic advantages of having many sons and no daughers, the
student said the family had economic problems which his parents
blamed on the fact that the two older brothers did not remain in
the extended family. The mother had a tubectomy following an
unplanned pregnancy, the baby having died at birth.

Our family faces the problem of money shortage
because we have a large family to maintain.

I have never heard my mother talk about the problems
of a large family, but I have heard my father tell
a friend with ten children, "You could live better
if you did not have so many." He says a large
family is not good because it taxes the earning
members too much. My father believes that too
many children is a problem but he also thinks that
without a large family it would be difficult to continue
living, so what can one do? Many people have
financial difficulties with a large family like ours
even though all the children are sons.

I don't know what my mother thinks but she had a
sterilization operation after her last delivery.

Scheduled Castes and Tribes

Of the eight students in this group, all said that the family
had economic problems and some were existing at a subsistence
level. The average number of living children was 5.0 and no
family had fewer than two living sons. All of the students were

aware of the problems of relatively large families. Half of this group indicated direct expression on the part of the parents while the other half indicated indirect communication of the need to control family size.

<u>No parental discussion but apparent communication of the need for control of family size.</u> With the father the only source of income, and four sons to educate, the boy who had tribal ancestry said he believed his father would regard having fewer children as a better situation but he had not discussed it with him. One youth from a scheduled caste lived in the school dormitory and although he said he had not discussed the subject with his family, he was aware that both an elder brother and sister had been sterilized to keep from having more children. In another case, the pressures of a large family were evident to the students in spite of the lack of a direct discussion.

Scheduled Tribe Male (Case 30). There were five children in the family, four sons (ages 8, 10, 14, and 17), and one daughter (age 21). When the mother died, the married sister, husband and two children moved in with the family, a traditional custom of Bhils not usually practiced by families of other castes and communities. The father and son-in-law worked as farm day laborers and their combined income was about Rs. 800 per year. The student seemed aware of the problems caused by having too many people in a family although there was no indication of discussions with his father about the subject.

> We are four sons but we are still young and dependent on my father. Our family income is not sufficient and we have economic problems. Our father has to over-strain because of this. My mother is dead so my sister and her family stay with us. They help us but their presence also results in extra costs.

> I feel my father is disturbed by the poor condition of our family and he thinks as I do. With a small family one can provide good food and attention to all the children. Better health can be maintained. If the family is small, as much education as the children want can be provided. Also one can enjoy some luxuries such as good clothing.

Scheduled Caste Male (Case 34). There were five children in the family, three sons (ages 16, 25, and 30), and two daughters (ages 22 and 35). All were married except the student. The father was dead and the mother lived in the city with the eldest son. The second son also lived in the city with his family. Both sons worked for the railway with annual salaries of about Rs. 700 a year. The two daughters lived with their husbands in villages near Varna. The student lived in a dormitory provided by the government for scheduled caste and tribe students. Although he had had no discussion with his parents about family problems, the boy was aware of economic problems related to family size and reported that both a brother and a sister had terminated their fertility by operations. The oldest brother had a vasectomy after fathering two sons, and the married sister had had a tubectomy after having three children.

> We are a poor family without enough income. It is
> difficult now to meet the needs of a large family.
> My friends consider it a great problem. Sometimes
> they have to starve.

> My father and mother rarely talked to me. I do
> not know what their views were of family life.
> They did believe that children should be well
> educated. As I told you, I do know that one brother
> and one sister have been sterilized.

Scheduled Caste Male (Case 35). There were five children in the family, three sons (ages 13, 16, and 18), and two daughters (ages 20 and 25). The two daughters were married. One of the daughters stayed with the family along with her three young children. The eldest son had recently been married and his 15-year-old wife had come to live with the family. The family lived on the income of the father from farm labor which was estimated to be about Rs. 400 a year. While the problems of the family were discussed, family size was not mentioned directly. However, the boy believed, from comments his parents had made, that they would have preferred to have had fewer children.

> My family has many problems. There is the
> problem of food for all of us. Our family has only
> a small amount of money so it is difficult to manage
> on such a limited income. My father works hard

to support the family.

Family problems are talked of. The problem
most talked about is the shortage of food grains
and the lack of money. The education of the
children is also a source of worry. The size of
the family is not discussed directly, but references
are made, such as, "The family is so big we cannot
make ends meet. " I think my parents now realize
what the consequences of having a large family
are. I think they would have liked a smaller family
but no effort was made to do that. They now think
that a smaller family would mean more food, fewer
quarrels... there would be fewer persons to share
the same income.

Scheduled Caste Male (Case 36). There were seven
children in the family, four boys (ages 17, 18, 22, and 27), and
three girls (ages 4, 7, and 12). The two eldest sons were
married and lived in the extended family with their wives and
children. The only family member with a steady job was the
oldest son who worked in a mill. All of the other adults, father,
sons and their wives, followed the traditional occupation of
agricultural field work for one of the large landowners for daily
wages between Rs. 1. 50 and 2. 00. The family income was about
Rs. 900 per year. The student said he was aware of his parents'
concern about the size of the family and their economic
difficulties, but that problems of family size were not discussed
openly.

We have to undergo great financial stress. We
all have to work to have enough income. We also
borrow money by getting a loan from the mill where
my brother works. My father is getting old now
and worries about not being able to work.

The size of our family is not discussed in my
presence. My mother and father worry about having
so many children but my father does not discuss
it with me.

Expressed need for control of family size. In three of the four
families where the parents expressed a need for family planning,

the income was from wages earned as farm labor. The consistent problem in these families was not only the inadequate wages in regard to rising prices, but the fact that it seemed to be more difficult to find work than it was in the past. One father had steady steady work as a servant but, again, the income was clearly inadequate to support his family.

Scheduled Caste Male (Case 29). There were six children in the family, four sons (ages 5, 8, 17, and 20), and two daughters (ages 3 months and 3 years). The mother and father worked as farm laborers but had recently been unable to find regular employment. In spite of the fact that the eldest brother had completed the SSC (11th Standard), he had been unable to find a job. The parents had discussed family problems and the need for having a small family but the mother had just given birth to a daughter and no mention was made of the use of any family planning method.

> We have a large family and a shortage of cash.
> There are eight persons in the family who are
> dependent on Rs. 30 a month. My parents have
> worked for the Zamindar, but now they often do
> not get work. Too many people are living in the
> village which is a problem for people like my
> parents. My father said that in the past the
> Zamindar would regularly call on our family to
> work on his land. Now there are many people
> for him to call. They call to work only favored
> persons and now also they don't have to pay as
> much. That is why I want to be a teacher, and
> have a steady income. Teachers are not dependent
> on the landlords and so there is more security.

> My brother passed his SSC but he cannot study
> beyond secondary school because there is no
> money. This may also be my problem.

> My father and mother always talk about the
> problems of having so many children. When
> they do not get work they talk like this. They
> say that if they had a small family, they could
> save part of the income and use it during difficult
> times.

Scheduled Caste Male (Case 31). There were four children in the family, two sons (ages 7 and 17), and two daughters (ages 2 and 4). The father had a "service" job (servant) and earned Rs. 700 a year. The economic difficulties of the family were severe although it was a steady income compared with farm labor work. The problems of family size had been discussed in the student's home.

> Our family does have an economic problem and
> we have had had to take a loan from the provident
> fund. Sometimes we do not get enough to eat.
> My parents also worry abour education and marriage
> for my brother and me.

> My parents do talk about the size of the family.
> My father and mother believe that a small family
> is a happy family. One day our neighbor was forced
> to sell his kitchen utensils and a section of his
> steel roof because he did not have enough money
> for food for his seven children and he could not
> feed them. So my parents talked one night about
> the need to limit family size and they referred
> to this family as an example.

Scheduled Caste Male (Case 32). There were five children in the family, three sons (ages 2, 11, and 17), and two daughters (ages 15 and 22). The two daughters were married and living with their husbands. The student had just been married. The father was a farm day laborer with a yearly income of about Rs. 400, but had found it increasingly difficult to find steady work. Family size was discussed in their home and the mother had had a tubectomy following the birth of her last child.

> Poverty is the biggest problem in our family.
> One day my father gets work and the next day he
> is unemployed. So many times our family has not
> eaten for days. No one will lend us money because
> we can't pay it back.

> My mother and father always talk about all the
> children and the problems of educating us all.
> As I said, they even have trouble feeding us.

They have said that having fewer children might
have helped us to avoid this poverty. Now my
mother has had a sterilization operation.

Scheduled Caste Male (Case 33). There were four
children in the family, two sons (ages 7 and 17), and two
daughters (ages 5 and 11). The father died and the children
lived with their mother and their father's mother. The major
source of the family's income was the wages of the mother who
worked as a day laborer in the fields of the landowners of the
village. Her yearly cash income was not over Rs. 400 and since
field work was seasonable, there were periods when there was
no income at all. As a result, the family was often forced to
borrow money. The eldest son was attending school on
government funds. Even so, this was a hardship for the family
since the boy could only work part-time. The sacrifice was being
made in the hope that having completed the 11th Standard, he
would be able to elevate himself above the traditional occupation
of farm laborer, with its low and unsteady income. The boy was
well aware of family problems and his mother had told him to
have a small family.

My father died so we have no male who is an
earning member of our family. We manage on
the little my mother earns as a field laborer.
We borrow money to live, then we pay back the
money lenders when my mother works. This
never ends so I will be unable to go further with
my education.

My mother does talk about family size. She
has told me I should get a job first and then
marry. She has said, "If you want a good living,
you must have a small family."

Conclusion

A major purpose of the study has been to determine the
kinds of influence families may have had on the students in terms
of forming and modifying their beliefs regarding family size and
the control of family size. It was assumed that economic
variables would be one of the more important determining factors

Table 6. Summary of Assessment of Parental Expression Regarding Family Size Limitation from Student Comments by Sex and Status Groupings

Parental Expression	Higher Caste				Lower Castes & Communities		Total	
	Males		Females		Males			
	N	%	N	%	N	%	N	%
Direct or indirect communication of the need to control family size	9	64	4	31	11	92	24	62
Parental ambivalence regarding control of family size	0	0	6	46	0	0	6	15
No parental discussion of family size	2	14	0	0	1	8	3	8
Parental preference for a large family or opposed to control	3	22	3	23	0	0	6	15
Total	14	100	13	100	12	100	39	100

in such parental communication. The families from which the students came were divided into those from high castes with no stated problems, those from high castes with stated problems but not directly economic in nature, those from high castes with economic problems, those from lower caste families and those from scheduled castes and scheduled tribes.

We attempted to assess the expression of parental feelings regarding family size from the comments made by the students to questions throughout each interview.

Distribution by case number and number of children is given in Table 5. Table 6 is a summary of these data where the ratings of parental expression have been reduced to four categories: direct or indirect communication of the need to control family size, parental ambivalence regarding control of family size, no parental discussion of family size, parental preference for a large family or opposed to control.

For the total sample of students, 62 percent were rated as living in families where there was evidence of either direct or indirect communication of the need to control family size. In 15 percent of the cases there seemed to be parental ambivalence regarding control of family size. In eight percent of the cases no parental discussion of family size was indicated. In 15 percent of the cases there was a stated parental preference for a large family or an indication of opposition to family size control.

Although the number of cases does not permit the claim of statistical significance, it is interesting to note the difference between the responses of students from high caste families and those from lower castes and communities. Of those students from the lower castes and communities, all but one student indicated either direct or indirect parental communication of the need to control family size while less than half of the high caste students did so. The only students to indicate parental preference for a large family or being opposed to family size control were from higher caste families. In only two of the six cases in this category (Cases 2 and 39) might this be attributed to the lack of sons (Table 5). However, a good share of this difference is accounted for by the differential responses of the higher caste boys and girls. Only four of the 13 girls indicated either direct or indirect communication with parents regarding the need to control family size, and Table 5 shows that only one girl stated this as an overt parental expression. These findings would suggest the possibility of less parental communciation among the higher castes than among lower caste and low status community groups, and less parental communcation for higher caste girls than for higher caste boys.

The findings in this section suggest that the majority of the families of the youth in this study were under economic strain. This is hardly a new finding for an Indian village. There was, however, reason to believe that economic problems were regarded as increasing, particularly for families in the lower socioeconomic strata and that a majority of parents had communicated some recognition to the sons and daughters in the study that large families increased the economic burden.

What did this learning mean when translated into desired number of children? In the next section we will examine the personal family size desires of the youth based on how they viewed the advantages and disadvantages of large and small families as a result of what they had experienced in their own families and how ideal family size may be changing.

V. Family Size Attitudes

The value of having many children has traditionally been stressed in Hindu society as it has in most peasant cultures. Girls at the time of their wedding were still often blessed with, "May you have a thousand sons. " Basically, the socialization practices which emphasized the bearing of children had not changed. A girl still learned that the only way she could gain power and status in the family of her husband was by having enough sons so that at least one lived. She could expect to move from the position of the shy, retiring young girl who must minister to the every need of the family members of her in-laws to the all-powerful and controlling mother-in-law; but obviously, that can be done only through sons. Sons were also important to the males for help with farm work, to perform rituals and also for status reasons; but more importantly, for security when the elders were no longer able to support themselves.

Still, when the responses to the questions asking about the advantages and disadvantages of small and large families were tabulated, the 49 students were able to give more reasons for a small family (defined as two children) than they could for a large family (defined as five children). There was a total of 2.0 responses pointing to the advantages of a small family and .7 advantages of a large family. This was consistent with the responses of adult villagers who also gave a greater number of advantages for a small family than they did for a large one (Poffenberger and Poffenberger, 1973; Poffenberger, 1975).

The Advantages of a Small Family

The type of responses given by the youth were also consistent with those given by the adults. The most common given for the advantage of a small family was economics. Of the students 61 percent mentioned that the cost of food, clothing and other needs would be less with a small family. In addition, 23 percent mentioned other financial benefits such as fewer marriage costs and being able to save more money for old age.

As with the adult samples, the advantage next in frequency had to do with health of the mother and children,

63

mentioned by 54 percent of the students. As might be expected with this group of young people, educational opportunities were mentioned next in frequency (44 percent). Sixteen of the students (41 percent) also indicated a belief that a small family was generally happier with fewer conflicts and worries.

The comments of a high caste girl (Case 8) indicate the concern regarding ability to provide basic needs and health concerns. A lower caste boy (Case 33) stressed the economic aspects.

> The main disadvantage of a large family is that
> there will be a shortage of clothes and food.
> Proper treatment for any sick members would
> be difficult because of a shortage of resources.
> There isn't enough room and money to care
> adequately for the sick. You could not buy things
> according to your free will. You would always
> have to consider the other members of the family
> when you want to buy something.

> To my mind, a small family involves fewer
> expenses. More care can be provided for children
> in a smaller family. For example, if we have
> one pound of milk and two children, then each
> child can get one-half pound of milk. The same
> argument can be applied in various other matters.
> So, a small family is better. I told you the story
> where the whole family met destruction because
> there were too many children. Thus I know that
> a small family is better than a large family.
> There would be less burden on the part of the
> earning members of a small family.

Examples of comments regarding the advantage of education, better child training, less work for the mother and the reduced possibility of family conflicts were mentioned by a girl (Case 5) and a high caste boy (Case 21).

> You can give the members of a small family
> proper education. It is possible to teach good
> values because of the greater attention you can
> pay each member. You can live in peace.

There is good health for the children and the
mother.

I feel small families have a lot of advantages.
In a small family, one can live happily. Education
of children will not be a bother or expensive.
The health of the children will remain good.
You can spend money on entertainment in a
small family. You can pay proper attention to
each member of the family.

The Advantages of a Large Family

We have said that the students gave an average of 2.0
responses to the open-ended question asking the advantages of
a small family and that the results were consistent with the adult
sample. In that study husbands had mentioned 2.8 and the wives
2.6 advantages of a small family. The students mentioned an
average of .7 advantages while husbands mentioned 1.0 and
wives 2.2 advantages of a large family. A village study in
North India reported similar findings. Asking the same
questions and using similar coding categories, Mani (1971) found
that 66 husbands and wives gave an average of 3.1 responses
and 40 wives gave an average of 3.4 responses favoring a small
family while both husbands and wives gave an average of only
one response to the question regarding the advantages of a large
family. We do not suggest that these findings indicate a small
family size norm predominates for these people. As we have
reported previously (Poffenberger, 1975), when villagers talked
of the advantages of a small family they spoke of the problems
of childbearing and rearing, and these were the pressures at the
time of the interviews. When they talked of a large family, they
were thinking primarily of the advantages to be gained later in
the life cycle when fathers could no longer work or when mothers
might be widowed and this one variable may be more significant
than all the low fertility motives together.

For the students, as with the adults, economic reasons
predominated in stating the need for a large family. Four said
a large family can earn more money. One said that money could
be saved by buying large quantities in wholesale lots. A girl
(Case 1) stated the importance of sons as a source of income.

Well, I think because of the economic burden
a small family would be better. But, there is
nothing really bad about a large family. A son
is essential; even more than one son, to help
earn money for the family. Sons also help to
look after you in your old age. Girls are more
of a problem. Still a daugher is also necessary.
She can work around the house and be of help
to the mother.

Seven students, as with one Scheduled Caste boy (Case
35), stated that a big family provided more hands to do the work.

In farming, a large family is an asset. You
don't have to keep servants to help, so it is
economical with a large family. If someone gets
sick in a large family, then he can receive better
care.

Examples of the importance given to companionship were
stated by both a girl (Case 12) and a Scheduled Caste boy
(Case 30).

As I've said before, the fun of living together
is one thing good about a large family. We are
all fond of singing and enjoy singing together.
We hardly feel like going out because we are such
a good group. One would get help in the household routines with a large family.

With a large family, each member can live in
the company of each other.

The constant fear of loss of children among villagers was
also reflected in the comments of five students such as the
remarks made by two girls (Cases 5 and 39).

In a small family, if the children should die,
then who would look after the parents in their
old age ?

If there is an epidemic our children die and then
we are left alone to work for the rest of our lives.

Desired Numbers of Sons and Daughters

The students stated more advantages to a small family than to a large family yet many still saw advantages in a large family. How many, then, did they actually want?

The question of validity needs to be raised when asking about desired numbers of children. In our interviews with village men and women over a period of years, it has been evident that they were seldom clear in their own minds as to just what number of children is best. The response of a village woman might vary between two or three and five children in the same interview. The response of our students to a question asking about ideal numbers could hardly be regarded as any more reliable. The question, however, provides a point of departure for an examination of the values of sons and daughters. It also provides at least some indication of response differences between men and women and between groups, as well as generational differences.

In the earlier study of families, we found that there was a difference both in terms of the responses of the older and younger generations and in terms of husband-wife responses within each generation. Table 7 (next page) shows that for mothers with an average of 4.4 living children and 35.4 years of age, believed that 2.5 sons and 1.4 daughters would be ideal. The fathers indicated a desire for fewer children, with an average of 1.8 sons and 1.3 daughters. A sample of young husbands and wives in the village, where the mothers' average age was 19.4 indicated a desire for fewer children. The wives said they would prefer 1.9 sons and 1.1 daughters while the husbands stated a desire for 1.6 sons and 1.2 daughters. It is clear that for both the older and younger generation, there was a clear preference for sons, although the over-all numbers were less for both sons and daughters with the younger people.

As we will see, the responses of our students were not greatly different. They did want fewer children on the average, than did the young married men and women, but largely because they indicated a desire for fewer girls. The desire for sons remained very nearly the same for both groups.

In order to determine how important it was to have a son,

Table 7

Average Number of Living Children and Number Said to Be Ideal by Samples of Older Mothers and Fathers and Young Husbands and Wives from the Same Extended Families in a Village near Varna.#

Sex of Children	Mothers and Fathers*			Young Husbands and Wives**		
	Living	Ideal for Mothers	Ideal for Fathers	Living	Ideal for Wives	Ideal for Husbands
		N=66	N=60		N=30	N=33
Males	2.5	2.5	1.8	.5	1.9	1.6
Females	1.9	1.4	1.3	.4	1.1	1.2
Total Children	4.4	3.9	3.1	.9	3.0	2.8

*The average age of mothers in the sample was 35.4 years.

**The average age of the wives in the sample was 19.4 years.

#Adapted from T. Poffenberger, Fertility and Family Life in an Indian Village, Michigan Papers on South and Southeast Asia, 10 (Ann Arbor: CSSEAS Publications, 1975).

69

Table 8

Average Number of Children in Family of Origin and Number Desired in Family of Procreation by High Caste Boys and Girls and Lower Caste and Community Boys.

Sex of Children	Children in Family of Origin				Children Desired in Family of Procreation			
	High Caste Females	High Caste Males	Lower Caste and Community Males	Total	High Caste Females	High Caste Males	Lower Caste and Community Males	Total
	N=13	N=14	N=12	N=39	N=13	N=12*	N=12	N=37
Males	2.4	3.1	3.1	3.0	1.9	1.8	1.7	1.8
Females	2.2	1.6	2.1	2.0	.9	.4	.6	.6
Total Children	4.5	4.7	5.2	5.0	2.8	2.2	2.3	2.4
Maximum children students would have to have a son					4.0	3.2	2.8	3.4

*Two male students did not answer as they said they did not plan to marry.

we also asked how many children they would have, if all were girls, in order to have a son. While some of the students indicated that they would stop at the number they wanted regardless of the sexes of the children, many more stressed the importance of having additional children to have a boy.

If boys are so much more important than girls to village families, why is this so? In this section we have also reviewed the responses of the students to questions asking what their mothers and fathers thought were the advantages and disadvantages of sons and daughters.

The average number of children desired for the total sample was only 2. 4. However, while the high caste boys and the lower castes and communities boys wanted 2. 2 and 2. 3 children respectively, the girls wanted 2. 8.

The total sample stated an average desire for 1. 8 males and only . 6 females. There was a sex difference in desire for females, and the greater desire for females on the part of the girls made the difference in the overall larger number of children desired by the girls. While both boys and girls wanted nearly two boys on the average, the girls wanted an average of . 9 girls while the high caste males and lower castes and communities boys stated a preference for . 4 and . 6 girls respectively. These figures have been placed along side the number of children in the families of the students for comparison (Table 8). The average number of children desired by the students (2. 4) is considerable smaller than the number in their own families (5. 0).

However, the expressed desire for sons would seem to require considerable modification in the 2. 4 figure in terms of eventual fertility behavior. When we examined their comments regarding the maximum number of children they would have in order to have a son, the average family size was increased to 3. 4. [4]

There were also differences between the boys and girls in the number they would have before stopping in order to have a male. The girls on the average would not stop until they had four children. The high caste males, while desiring to stop well before the girls (3. 2), indicated they would be willing to have a larger total number of children than were the poorer lower castes and communities students (2. 8).

The comments of the girls clearly indicated the importance of sons. Four girls (Cases 1, 5, 9, and 10) indicated that a son was so necessary that one would continue to have children until a boy was born, in spite of the fact that each might prefer a small family.

> I think a small family is best, but at least one son is necessary. I cannot know how many children it would take.

> I would like to have three children, but a son is a must. I do not know how many children I could have, but I must have a son.

> I would like two or three children, but not more than four. However, a son is essential so if I had three daughters, I would hope for a son on the fourth pregnancy.

> Two children, a son and a daughter, are enough, but I must have a son. I will have an operation as soon as I have a son.

The rest of the girls said they would stop having children after a certain number even if they had no son. Two cases (Cases 7 and 39) said they would not go beyond five children.

> I would have two or three children, I think there should be two sons and a daughter. I can imagine having a maximum of five children. I would not want more than five children at any cost.

> I want three sons and one daughter. If my first four children were daughters, a fifth trial for a son is necessary. In no case would I have more than five children.

The remaining five girls (Cases 2, 3, 4, 6, and 11) said they would stop after three children.

> I would like to have two children, one son and
> one daughter. If both children were daughters,
> I would still want a son, but I would still stop
> after three daughters.

> I would want a boy and a girl. I would have only
> one more if both were girls.

> In no case do I want more than three children.
> I would certainly wish to have a boy. But if I
> had three girls, I would not try for a fourth.

> I would like two or three children. I want a son
> and a daughter, but will stop at three.

> I would like to have two children. If both were
> sons, then I would stop. I would want to have
> a third child, if the first two were daughters,
> but I do not want more than three.

As with the girls, most of the boys made it clear that
they preferred sons. Four high caste boys were particularly
strong in their feelings about the need for a son. Three simply
could not believe that they could not have a son (Cases 14, 27,
and 32).

> I would like to have only two children, both sons.
> I can't imagine not having a son. If all my children
> were girls, I would wait for a son and then I would
> get an operation.

> I would like to have two sons. I would be satisfied
> with no daughters. It is possible I would have
> one son and one daughter, but I cannot imagine
> not having a least one son. One at least must
> be a son. This is important.

> I would like two sons and no more children.
> This is all I'll have. I will have only boys.

However, Case 28, one of the two boys not wanting to
marry, seemed less concerned about not having a son than
avoiding having a wife and daughter.

Children? I told you I would definitely not
marry. If you tell me to just suppose, I would
have only <u>one</u> son. If the child were a girl, I
would desert her. I would not kill her. But I
would leave both a daughter and a wife with my
parents and go and serve in the city forever.

Three Scheduled Caste boys seemed to feel less strongly
about sons. However, Case 29 was certain that he would have
males.

I am sure that I will have sons because I am
strong. I want two sons. That is all.

The other three (Cases 30, 31, and 36) were willing to
give up after four daughters.

Two boys and a girl would be what I want. If
all three were girls, I would have one more,
but I would not have more than four.

If three children were all girls, I would try for
a fourth but not more than four.

At least one son must be there, but three
daughters and one son would do. I would not
have more than four.

Four other boys, two high caste, one lower caste and one
Scheduled Caste, seemed willing to give up sooner in their
desire for a son. The high caste boys were Cases 15 and 25.

If I have two daughters, I would try for one more
issue. If I did not get a male after three attempts,
I would like my wife sterilized.

I would like to have only two children. If both
of these were girls, I would try one more time.
If I happened to have three girls, I would stop.
A son is important, but not enough to continue
having more and more children. I know I can
take care of myself in later years. I can put
enough money aside for that.

74

The lower caste and the Scheduled Caste boys were Cases
18 and 35.

> I would like to have two sons. If I had two girls
> then I would try for only one more. I have no
> right to spoil the lives of the other children at
> the cost of some desire of mine.

> If the first two children are daughters, then I
> would like to try for a son, but three are the
> maximum number of children.

The remaining fourteen boys said they would not have
children beyond the number they wanted, to have a son. Even
though sons were still generally preferred over daughters, these
boys indicated daughters were also quite acceptable. The
following cases are from high caste families (Cases 16, 21, 23,
24, 26, and 37).

> I would like three children. This would fit nicely
> within the income I plan to have. I would like to
> have two sons and one daughter. I believe a son
> is important in the family, but this does not mean
> I should spoil the future of the other children by
> having more.

> I will have only two children. This means two.
> Not one, not three. If they are daughters it does
> not matter. I want a son, but only if he is within
> the number two.

> I would like to have two sons and a daughter.
> In case I would have all boys or even all girls,
> I would not mind. I want only three.

> I would like three, two sons and a daughter.
> I would be able to maintain three children and
> no more. If I have three sons, I would not like
> to have a fourth for a daughter. If I had three
> daughters, I would not have a fourth for a son.

> I would not marry. I would never marry. If
> under some circumstance I had to marry, I

would have only one or two children. It would
not matter if they were boys or girls.

I want two, a boy and a girl. I do not want less
than two and I will not have more than two no
matter what sexes.

I would like two sons. But if I had two baby girls
I would not try for a son. To me both sons and
daughters are the same. A daughter would marry
and reside with her in-laws. A son would make
his living on his own. Both would leave the
family in any case.

The following represent lower castes and communities
(Cases 17, 19, 20, 33, and 34) and indicate the importance of
economic restrictions for this group in their decision regarding
how many children to have in order to have a son.

I would like to have two sons or one son and one
daughter. In no case would I want more, even if
I had all girls. I say so because how can a large
family be maintained on a small income. I know
this condition very well because I have experienced
it.

I want only two children. I am very firm about
this. I don't care what their sex is. I don't
care if it is two sons or one son and one daughter
or two daughters. Two children are enough
these days.

I would like two. If I try for one more than I
would really have hardships. I would have to
feed too many. I will have a small income.
It does not matter if they are boys or girls.

If I have two girls, I would not try for more.
If I have only two, it would be easier for me to
look after these children.

I would like to have two children. I believe two
children, no matter whether sons or daughters,
are adequate.

One student, a high caste boy (Case 13), indicated that even if he did not have a son, a brother's son could meet extended family needs.

> I would like to have two sons, but even if the
> first two children were girls, I would not have
> more. My brother already has a son. This
> would be a matter of satisfaction to me and keep
> the lineage open.

The last student, another high caste boy (Case 38), suggested the adoption of his sister's son.

> If I have all girls, then I would not have another.
> We could adopt a son of our sister's. Once a
> family in our caste had no son, so they adopted
> a male child of their family. Now they live nicely.
> So I would not try for one more child after having
> two daughters. But I am very sure that I will
> have a son.

Conclusion

As with the older villagers in the region, the students gave more advantages for having a small family than they did for having a large family. The cost of rearing a family and the need to save money for marriages and one's old age were mentioned. Some said a small family was happier because there were fewer conflicts while others said there would be less work for parents. An important consideration was the health of both the mother and the children. On the other hand, there were also economic reasons given as an advantage of a large family. Sons as a source of income and as extra hands for field labor were mentioned. That a family with many children provided companionship and the fear that children may die were also given as reasons.

The students indicated a desire for fewer children of their own than in any previous study by the senior author in the area. However, the continued importance of sons was obvious. Of the 39 students, 25 said they would have additional children beyond the number they wanted, in order to have a son.

The group differences are worth repeating. The higher caste girls said they would not stop until they had had four children. The higher caste boys were willing to stop at 3.2 children, while the lower caste and community boys said they would stop at 2.8 children.

For all groups the value of sons may be the most important variable in maintaining relatively high fertility levels. We will look at this more closely in the next section.

VI. Advantages and Disadvantages
of Sons and Daughters

We have been interested in the possible influence of
parents in determining the attitudes of the students. We have
seen that over 60 percent of the students indicated either direct
or indirect communication to themselves from their parents
regarding the importance of family size control. In addition,
as a group, they also said they would have 3.4 children in order
to have a son. To understand the variables which may influence
the eventual fertility of these boys and girls, it is obviously
important to understand the relative value given to sons and
daughters and how these values were inculcated. We have some
clue in their responses to questions regarding the advantages of
sons and daughters as viewed by their parents and the general
approval of the students of these views.

Advantages and Disadvantages of
Daughters as Viewed by Parents

When the students were asked what their mothers and
fathers thought was good and bad about having a daughter, only
23 of the 39 students answered the question.

Of those who responded, fourteen indicated only a
negative attitude on the part of the parents, five indicated that
there were both advantages and disadvantages recognized and
four pointed only to advantages of a daughter. The advantages
had to do largely with the sharing of household responsibilities.
The disadvantages centered largely on the fear that a daughter
might disgrace the family by having premarital intercourse, the
difficulty and cost of arranging a satisfactory marriage and the
cost of raising a child who would be of benefit only to another
family.

The disadvantages were expressed by three high caste
boys (Cases 21, 24, and 28).

Having a daughter is not good to my father's way
of thinking. She will go away after marriage.

79

A lot of debt will arise from her marriage and
the problems may continue for her whole life.
If the husband is not good, her life will be ruined
and we will be hurt to witness it. My mother
feels the same way.

Having a daughter is a liability in any case.
You cannot rest in peace until she is married
according to my father.

My mother and father think a daughter produces
tension. She is a risk. She has to be married.
My father has to provide a dowry of about Rs.
7,000 at the time of marriage. And then there is
is no guarantee that she will be happy.

Even in the Scheduled Castes, where a bride price is paid
rather than a dowry, a daughter was still regarded as a problem
as indicated by Cases 35 and 36, both males.

A daughter, according to my father, is a source
of worry even though we do not have dowry. In
our caste, we get money from the boy's side.
To find a person, however, who will keep her
happy is difficult. In addition, she will go away
to some other place. She cannot be much of an
asset to the family.

A daughter is not so expensive to marry in our
caste because we have bride price which is paid
by the boy's father and not the girl's. But still
a daughter is a liability according to my father
because of the cost of raising her and because
she is a source of worry and tension.

However, two boys spoke only of the advantages of
daughters as viewed by their parents. A high caste boy (Case 22)
said his mother appreciated the help of her daughter around the
home.

My mother says about a girl that one is essential
to help me in the kitchen. She is called the
Laxmi (goddess of wealth) of the family.

A low caste boy (Case 30) pointed to the advantage of having a daughter to his own family.

> My father would feel good about having a
> daughter. It has its advantages. See, my
> mother is dead. This has left us alone. My
> sister had to come back to our house and take
> over the responsibilities of rearing my younger
> brothers.

Two of the girls (Cases 3 and 9) expressed the common view of the liabilities of girls without indicating any positive values.

> My mother feels that girls are someone else's
> property. She feels they have to be given away
> when they are grown up.

> A son is always an asset. He will earn and serve
> while a daughter is a liability and someone else's
> property. Girls can only work at home and incur
> expenses.

Three of the girls (Cases 6, 7, and 8) expressed the feeling of the their parents that while there were disadvantages to having daughters, there were also some advantages.

> My father does not curse girls. However, the
> money he must offer in marriage (dowry) may
> bother him sometimes.

> A good girl would help the mother. She would
> be docile and sweet. But she is also a liability.
> If she gets out of hand—well, the family's
> reputation is at stake.

> A daughter should be modest and not the out-
> going type. If she could study and earn an income
> she would be a definite asset to the family. But
> it would be worse than death to my father if a
> daughter turned the wrong way. What would be
> the consequences if she formed a habit of going
> out with boys? She would say she had gone to

her girl friend's. In fact, girls are a much greater
source of worry to a father than a son. A father
does not know what to do with his daughter. If
he does not encourage her to study, then he has
difficulty in arranging her marriage. If he
encourages her to study, then she might associate
with boys and create a problem. Either way, a
father takes a chance with a daughter. My mother
feels the same way.

Two girls (Cases 11 and 12), however, presented only a
positive view of a daughter.

One daughter is good to help the mother or to
bring variety to the family.

My father and mother feel that a family must
have both a son and a daughter. A daughter is
needed to share the problems of the mother.

Advantages and Disadvantages of
Sons as Viewed by Parents

The students were also asked what their mothers and
fathers though was good and bad about having a son. All of the
students expressed the advantages of having a son. The most
common was in terms of the economic benefit to the extended
family. Over 70 percent mentioned such things as adding to the
family income and providing care for parents in their old age.
Nine (24 percent) of the students mentioned the need of a son to
keep the family lineage open and to inherit family property.
Four of the girls, however, also indicated that there were
disadvantages to having boys. The disadvantages were largely in
terms of the sons not performing their duties according to the
traditional expectation after the investment of the early years
was made.

For the most part, the boys viewed their parents as
seeing sons as essential. As examples, we will quote three boys
from higher castes and three boys from lower castes and
communities.

The higher caste examples are Cases 14, 16, and 38.

My father believes a son should keep good support for him during old age and any sickness. A son would keep the family lineage open. He would perform the funeral ceremonies for his parents. I believe as my father believes regarding the importance of having a son. He would look after me in old age. He would perform the funeral ceremonies.

A son is necessary to perform religious ceremonies at the time of his parents' death. If either parent dies, he can take up the responsibility of his younger brothers and sisters. The oldest son has to perform the role of a father.

A son is important because he is an heir to the property. He can also look after his parents in their old age. If my mother had not had a son, on whom would she have depended for the support of her two daughters? What about their marriages? Who would perform religious ceremonies after their deaths? So I think a son is important in a family. My mother is always saying, 'I am living because you are there. Otherwise, how can I fight with life in such hard days.'

The lower castes and communities examples are Cases 17, 29, and 33.

My father believes a son is important to perform religious ceremonies after his death. A son is considered to be the heir of property.

My father believes it is good to have a son. In his old age a son would help him in all respects. He would provide money. He would look after both of them in sickness. He would take them on a religious pilgrimage.

My mother's life could be protected as long as

there is a son. If there is no son, then one must
save for his old age.

Most of the girls also said their parents viewed a son as
being vital to the family welfare (for example, Cases 1 and 9).

Oh, my father would see a son as essential.
A son can help earn for the family and take care
of the parents when they are old.

My parents see a son as important. He can even
go and earn in the city or another country like
Africa. Girls only incur expenses.

Several, however, pointed to problems sons might create
as in Cases 4 and 8.

Both my mother and father would wish for sons.
They would want more than one. If one did not
stay at home, the other would help the family.
My older brother did leave the family and this
has caused them great distress.

My father would think a son is more desirable
than a daughter only if the son had a good job
and earned a good income. He would expect a
son to care for him in old age and also care for
the brothers and sisters. A good son should
also take interest in his own children and educate
them properly. But it would be bad to have a
son turn out to be a vagabond. He might misuse
the property. He might misbehave and be bad
with girls. A son can also ruin the reputation
of the family.

The girl who lived alone with her mother (Case 39)
indicated that both she and her mother had rationalized the fact
that there was no son in the house.

My mother thinks it would be a risk to have a
son because he might not be as loyal to his mother
as a daughter is. A son might not understand
his mother. She might not be able to control him.

He might spend all the family money.

Advantages and Disadvantages of
Daughters and Sons as Viewed by Students

When the students were asked the advantages and disadvantages of sons and daughters, most of them said they agreed with their parents and simply repeated what they had expressed as their parents' beliefs. Two boys but none of the girls who said the parents saw no advantages in having a girl disagreed. One was a lower caste male (Case 17) who said:

> I do not agree with my father. He thinks a son is important because he will look after the duties that he cannot do. I don't believe in such an idea because if nobody is there to look after the parents, it should be given to the sister. Also, religious ceremonies can be performed by a member of the family.

The second boy, from a high caste, thought that girls could also be important if educated but added that a daughter would eventually have to leave the home (Case 24).

> I would disagree with my mother and father. There should be no difference between having a son or a daughter. If each child were properly educated then they could be of the same use to the family. But there is a difference because the girl would have to leave the family at some point.

Of interest regarding the response of the girls was the tendency to agree with the disadvantages of daughters to parents. Of the girls who said their parents saw only disadvantages in daughters, none disagreed.

Conclusion

The traditional value of sons was clearly expressed by the students both as they viewed their parents' attitudes and expressed their own. The disadvantages of having daughters was equally clearly expressed.

All 39 of the students said their parents saw advantages in sons and were able to mention one or more. On the other hand, only nine students mentioned advantages of daughters, five of them girls. Only two of the boys and none of the girls said they disagreed with their parents when the parents were regarded as seeing no advantage to having girls. From cost-benefit analysis, it was clearly more advantageous to have sons than daughters and these students, as their parents, will want to assure themselves of at least one son surviving them.

Still most of them say they will want to control their fertility and have smaller families than their parents had. We will look at their plans and concerns for the future and the family action possibilities that in part will determine the degree to which they may be able to have the number of children they want.

VII. Age at Marriage and Education

In this section we will examine how the students felt
regarding desired age at marriage, desired length of time before
having the first child and desired spacing between children. We
will then look at the possible relationship between increasing age
at marriage and education. An examination of the response of
the students provides us with an opportunity to view some of
their personal motives for wanting to change from traditional
patterns of early marriage, but more important, we will attempt
to go beyond the personal, and tie increasing age at marriage to
group desire for social status and economic gain through
education.

Desired Age at Marriage

The age at which husbands and wives begin living together
may have a significant impact on lowering fertility. Wyon and
Gordon (1971) attribute what decline they found in the Khanna
study to a change in age at marriage rather than to adoption of
family planning innovations. Traditionally age at marriage
in India has been considerably earlier than when the young
husband and wife actually begin living together. The girl is
generally not supposed to go to the home of her husband until
menarche. Although age at menarche varies widely both for
individuals and groups, the average age according to worldwide
samples seems to be about 15 years (Nag, 1968). What data we
were able to collect on age of first menstruation among village
girls would indicate that an average of 15 years was likely for
this region of India as well. The degree to which age at
marriage may be a contributing variable in fertility reduction
relates to adolescent sterility. Talwar (1965), using data from
the Singur study near Calcutta, found that at age 15 only about 60
percent of the girls were fecund. Fecundity increased to 78
percent by age 17 and by age 19 all the girls in the sample were
fecund. While estimates vary regarding how much the birthrate
may be reduced by increasing age of marriage for girls between
15 and 20, it seems likely that every year of increase beyond 17
is significant (Agarwala, 1966).

We did not obtain data from the students regarding the age their parents began to live together. However, our previous research in the region has indicated that for the age group of our students' mothers, the average was probably less than 15 years. Anker (1973) in his study of 470 couples in the area where Varna village is located found that of lower caste Baria females the age of effective marriage was 14.6 while for the high caste Patidar females it was 15.9 years.

For our sample of students, the girls said they regarded the best age to marry as 20.1 while the boys averaged 22.5. This is consistent with census data indicating a generally increasing age of marriage throughout India (Jain, 1967).

The advantage of a longer period for education was one of the reasons for delaying marriage given by two girls (Cases 12 and 39).

> Education and earning power should be considered.
> The cost of living is very high in these days.
> If a person gets married before he earns, it is
> an extra burden on the family. Good education
> is necessary for a good job. So, I feel a boy
> must complete his education. Twenty-five years
> should bring sufficient stability in this matter.
> For girls, basic education [completion of secondary
> school] is necessary. They should be trained
> in housekeeping. Therefore, twenty is the
> minimum age for a girl to marry.

> If a girl studies enough, she can have a job and
> earn. Early marriage interrupts one's study.
> Marrying early means increasing your responsi-
> bilities prematurely. This leads to family conflicts.

A high caste boy also related delayed age at marriage to education (Case 15).

> I think twenty-five is the best age. I would like
> to marry at this age so that I could take over
> responsibilities without taxing my parents. It
> would also help my education to marry at this
> age. If we are already married we cannot study.

> Once I am married I would have to look after my
> wife's affairs. If we marry at age twenty-five
> and wait two years to have a baby, then we can
> move freely and enjoy life.

Other reasons were also given for delaying marriage for
both boys and girls. Several girls specifically mentioned that
early marriage would lead to early parenthood (Cases 2 and 8).

> Twenty-one years is the best age to marry.
> The later you marry, the later you get children.
> One should marry only after one is mature and
> responsible enough for her additional responsibilities.

> I feel twenty-one to twenty-five is the best age
> for a girl to marry. If a girl marries at an earlier
> age she will get 'drowned' in the responsibilities
> of life. Her dreams will remain unfilled. She
> would not be able to go about with her friends.
> She would also start having children when she
> marries.

One girl (Case 2) said that if she waited until she was
twenty to marry, she would be able to remain longer in her
parents' home.

> I feel twenty years of age is an ideal age for
> girls to marry. This leaves good time to enjoy
> the carefree life at the girl's parents' place.

Another girl (Case 5) pointed out that fear and shyness
between a husband and wife made early marriage undesirable.

> I feel twenty-two is the best age for a girl, and
> twenty-five for a boy is all right. There is a
> lot of fear and shyness when a couple is young.
> Marriage after 18 will insure good health. My
> sister suffered a lot. She married when she
> was 14.

A boy stressed the added maturity with age (Case 21).

> I feel twenty-five is the best age for a boy to get
> married. The person should be mature enough.

He must know about life with his wife so that
he might behave properly. I mean that if one
is too young when married, he might obey his
friends' suggestions and not act humanely. He
might not know about the proper knowledge of
sex life with his wife.

However, the traditional value of earlier marriage was
still evident. A lower caste boy (Case 32) indicated the difficulty
in arranging the marriage of a girl if it was delayed too long.

Our sister married early because it is difficult
in our caste to keep a girl unmarried until she
is of an older age. If she waited until she was
old, no one would marry her.

This position was supported by a high caste girl (Case 9).

I feel that seventeen to eighteen years is the
best age for a girl to marry. It is difficult to
get a bridegroom after a girl crosses a certain
age limit.

Some also thought that boys should not delay marriage too
long. One boy pointed out that his mother would need the help of
a wife (Case 33).

The best age for a boy to marry would be twenty.
This way a boy's mother would not find any
difficulty. She would find a person to help her
if her son married. Also, in our community
most boys start earning an income by that age.

Two others said that if boys waited too long to marry they
would have premarital intercourse—a comment frequently made
by village parents regarding the need to marry daughters at an
early age, but a reason we never heard given for boys (Cases 19
and 26).

I think the age of 18 or 19 is all right. The reason
I think this is that many boys who do not get married
at that age turn to anti-social behavior. For
instance, in our village there are four women

who reside outside the village in a group of about
twenty families. These women are known to
invite men for sexual intercourse for money.
They also invite school children to come for
intercourse, if they can pay for it. These women
have diseases. Right in our village I know of
married women who invite boys to their house
for intercourse when their husbands are away.
So I think perhaps an early marriage is best.

I think sixteen to twenty is the best age for a
boy to marry. Marrying at this age keeps us
from going to a prostitute. An unmarried boy
is likely to take part in certain activities that
are harmful. One of my village friends has a
disease because he went to a prostitute.

Desired Length of Time before
Having the First Child

The importance of having a child soon after marriage has
traditionally been stressed in rural Indian families. We, therefore, asked how soon after living with a spouse would they like to
have their first child. Less than twenty percent said that they
would have a child soon after marriage; twenty-two percent said
they would not want to wait more than two years. However,
forty-six percent said they would like to wait two years or more.
The rest of the students said they did not know.

Most of those who wanted a child soon after marriage
indicated the recognition a couple would get and the satisfaction
children would bring parents as stated by Case 29.

I would prefer a baby soon after marriage. I
feel this way because my parents would then be
able to see our child and derive much happiness
from it.

Most of those who wanted to delay having children
mentioned economic advantages. However, some of the girls
stated that they would prefer to wait two or more years after
marriage for the first child to enjoy a period of freedom from

children and to adjust to new family responsibilities (Cases 1, 11, and 25).

> Not soon after marriage. I think one should
> be given time to get used to married life. I
> think at least not until after two or three years.

> Two years are necessary in order to adjust to
> married life; also, for freedom from the
> responsibilities of children during this period.

> I think I would not like to have my first child
> until at least two or three years after marriage.
> I think a couple ought to enjoy married life for
> a few years without the bother of children.

Desired Spacing Between Children

Village men and women are often regarded as having little understanding of the possibility of spacing or the advantages of it. However, when the students were asked if they would like to have a period of time between children, there was almost complete agreement that there should be two or three years between children. Only six students indicated that less than two years would be enough.

One high caste boy said he would delay his first child and wait until the child was in school before having a second (Case 38). 38).

> I want to have two children. I would wait until
> I am settled before I had my first child. I would
> like to wait six years before I had a second child.
> This way the oldest child would go to the Balwadi
> [nursery school] and not disturb the baby. This
> would relieve my wife from paying attention to
> both children at one time.

Many of the students gave as reasons for spacing, the fact that better care of the children would be possible and the mother's health would be protected (Cases 23 and 29).

I would like to keep a space of several years
between children so that my wife would recover
from her weaknesses and deficiences caused by
pregnancy. This would allow us to have a healthy
child each time.

I would like to keep a spacing of two years.
After two years, my wife would have no trouble
in looking after her second baby.

Years of Education Desired for
Sons and Daughters

The students generally viewed each generation obtaining
more education than the one before. The number of years of
education the parents had was minimal. Even for the high caste
families which reported no economic problems, the average
years of education for fathers was 8.1 and for mothers only 2.0
years. For the high caste group with economic problems, the
education level for fathers averaged 4.8 years and for mothers
2.0 years. The parents of students from lower castes and
communities had virtually no education (Table 9).

Table 9

Number of Years of Education of Students' Parents for
High Caste with No Stated Economic Problems, High Caste
with Economic Problems, and Lower Castes and Communities.

	High Caste No Economic Problems	High Caste Economic Problems	Lower Castes and Communities	Average
	N=14	N=13	N=12	N=39
Father	8.1	4.8	1.0	4.8
Mother	2.5	2.0	.7	1.8

With this background, the educational level of the students was significant although most believed they would not be able to continue further for economic reasons. It was clear, however, that they would like their children to go further than they did—some hoping that they would complete college.

The importance of higher education for some of the high caste boys was seen as leading to professional careers as in Case 21.

If my children are competent enough, I will make them doctors or pleaders [lawyers] . I have a reason for this. If I study more than my father did, my children will go further. My reputation will increase and they will be happy.

A lower caste boy (Case 19) indicated that the family hopes that each generation would go further in school.

I would like my children to be educated even more than I plan for myself. I think I would be able to help with their education even if they want to go for 15 years or more. I am planning for the education of my children. My father also wants this. He has already said that my son must get even more education than is planned for me.

A Scheduled Caste boy (Case 29) hoped his son would be able to complete college.

I would definitely want my son to have 11 years of education. If I could afford it, I would like him to be a graduate of a university.

Another Scheduled Caste boy (Case 32) mentioned the desire to have his son have enough education to become a teacher.

I would like my sons to be educated up to 13 years. I would like them to take the teacher's diploma course and become teachers. If a son is educated, it is good for him and his children.

I would have no problem paying for their education
as I think of a small family.

In general, the students did not regard education as
necessary for girls as for boys. This is clear in the comments
of three high caste boys (Cases 14, 15, and 25).

I would like my son to be educated, even further
than 13 years. The day-to-day value of education
is increasing all the time. I would not educate
my daughter as much. Girls are expensive to
a family. An investment like education doesn't
pay off in the future.

I would like my son to have 15 years of schooling.
He could then make his living nicely. He would
not have to depend on me in the future when I
am older. In my old age I would have the advantage
of his income. A daughter does not need so much
education. I would not allow a daughter to study
further. In our caste, a girl does not usually serve
[employment]. So, I would like her to be educated
enough so that she can read and write.

I would like my son to complete at least 15 years
of education. If he wanted to study further, I
would support him. I don't think it is of any use
for a girl to become educated. After all, they
do not have to find employment anywhere. Why
should they need education?

The belief that a girl need not have too much education
was even more pronounced in the lower socioeconomic groups,
as indicated by the comments of Case 34.

I would like my sons to be educated for 11 years
up to SSC. After completing this schooling,
they must serve and earn an income so that my
income can be complemented. I believe a daughter
should be educated up to 4th or 5th standard in
Gujarati medium. She only needs to learn to
read and write. That's enough. It wouldn't pay
to provide any more because we would not get

any return for educating her further. She would
not return any income to the family. Also, if
she were too well educated, we could not get a
suitable mate for her in our caste.

However, some students saw education for girls as a
value as well as for boys. One high caste boy (Case 16) said
education for girls was insurance against being left unsupported
by a husband.

I would want a son educated for 15 years. This
would be enough to earn a good income. If he
is well educated, he would earn more. I would
also like my daugher educated for 15 years.
This way she might not have to face any difficulty,
if she met with some unexpected accident,
widowhood, for example. If she is educated,
she would be in a position to educate her children.
She could also take care of herself and her children.

A lower caste boy (Case 18) saw the education of a girl as
a help in obtaining a good husband as well as making it possible
to get a job.

I would like my children to be educated up to
15 years. If they are educated, they will have
good incomes. Education for a daughter is useful
because she would have a good mate. If she
serves then she will have additional income to
support her in-law's family.

Conclusion

Any delay in marriage beyond 17 or 18 years for girls in
the region can be expected to have a direct effect on fertility
since many will be fecund by that age. The average age of the
girls in the study was over 17 years and the average desired age
of marriage was 20. While these girls represented a select
group in the village, the reasons they gave for wanting to delay
marriage will likely influence others on a personal level. They
mentioned the advantages of additional years of freedom before
the responsibilities of marriage. Given the anticipated

difficulties in the family of their in-laws, the desire for delay is understandable.

These girls, however, regardless of personal desire, would not have been able to delay their marriage unless it was viewed as an advantage to the extended family. We have seen that delays in arranging the marriage of a daughter are chancy. The longer one waits the more likely it is that she will become involved with a boy, and any rumor of that sort reduces her value in the marriage bartering process. It is also said that the younger a girl is when she comes to the house of her mother-in-law, the easier it is to control her and train her to the expected patterns of behavior in the new setting.

Why, then, are these girls from the higher castes unmarried? The common answer is because they are still in school and custom has it that one does not marry until completing school. This line of reasoning leads to the conclusion that education is an important variable in fertility because, in part, of the role it plays in delayed marriage. As a result, one of the common recommendations for lowering fertility is to increase the length of time girls go to school. However, in the region of the study, as in India in general, this has not been done simply by providing more schools. The opportunities for girls already present are not fully used. We have mentioned previously that as of 1973, for all of India, only 12 percent of girls compared with 30 percent of boys ages 14 to 17 are enrolled in school (Nortnan and Hofstatter, 1975). Nor is interest in education for girls increasing as fast as for boys even though there is clear indication of increasing enrollment for both sexes. Our records of the village school for standards (grades) V through XI show an increase in enrollment between 1965-66 and 1968-69 of 40 percent for boys and 33 percent for girls. This increase for girls is accounted for largely by girls from higher caste families. The increase for boys, on the other hand, is due largely to increasing numbers enrolling from lower castes and communities. A major reason for families encouraging education at the secondary level for boys has been greater earning ability, an obvious advantage for parents who will depend on sons to care for them in older age. But daughters go to the home of their in-laws and are of little help in support of their own parents. Why then, when parents complain about the cost of rearing a girl, is education for girls increasing?

In a review of the literature on increasing age at marriage for girls in India, Mandelbaum (1975) concluded that it may be due to the emulation of the standards of late marriage set by educated people. From our studies it is clear that the increase in education for girls was in part due to the demand for well educated girls in marriage by boys from high caste families.

We have previously cited an example of one wealthy land-owner who had to build a secondary school in his village in order that his daughter could acquire the necessary education for a successful completion of the marriage arrangement and at the same time not be spoiled by attending school outside the village. Therefore, while the stress on education for boys has been largely based on economic advantages to the family, education for girls seems related to status considerations and the changing requirements of what is valued in the marital exchange. But these changes in values among the upper castes are important. As we have seen, since the highest status goes to those families who are able to marry their daughters into families where education is prized for boys and girls, the values held by these families are important to emulate. The question then of the degree to which education may be a variable in fertility decline is unclear as far as youth in the region of study is concerned. One thing is clear, the high castes such as the Patidars are not achievement-oriented because they are generally well-educated. Rather, the many schools in the region were built by the Patidars and other high castes because they were already achievement-oriented. Neither did their fertility rates decline because of education. The Census indicates fertility was declining for the caste long before most of the secondary schools were constructed. [5] There is considerable evidence to support the importance of caste in degree of achievement motivation. Nair (1961), for example, has pointed to the wide variation in drive for economic success on the part of the high caste Patidars and the lower caste Barias in the region. Hogle (1972), in a study of the same area, found caste the most important variable in the adoption of agricultural innovations as did Anker (1973) in terms of the adoption of family planning innovations.

Our conclusion would be that education is not the major motivating variable for lower fertility. Lower fertility among the higher castes may in fact only be an artifact of achievement motivation. In order to obtain status by having a daughter marry into a 'good' family, she must graduate from secondary school, and this results in delayed marriage and lower fertility.

This in no way should minimize the importance that education can play in reinforcing low fertility variables. Nearly 50 percent of the students said they would like to wait two years or more before having their first child and there was almost complete agreement that there should be two or three years between children. In addition to encouraging spacing, the schools may play the role they can do best, teach skills—and the skills that will have the greatest payoff in lowering fertility will be those which teach how fertility is best controlled.

Our data, however, provide us with no reason to assume the schools in the area will be able in themselves to create the desire to have fewer children. To the extent that these motives are learned, they will be inculcated as a result of the socialization process which takes place in the extended family and are reinforced by caste and community norms.

We will look next at the kinds of plans and concerns these students have regarding the future and then look at the situation variables after marriage which will in part determine the extent to which they will be able to have the number of children they want. These two sections will provide further understanding of the importance of socialization and the extended family in controlling the behavior of younger family members.

VIII. Life Planning and Concerns for the Future

What kind of problems did the young people expect to face after marriage? To plan an effective population education program for village youth we believed it was necessary to develop as much understanding as possible about how they saw the future and to what extent family size was viewed as important to them in any planning they might have considered. We first asked about the kinds of problems they thought they might encounter after they were married and, then, if the control of family size might be one of them.

Problems the Students Expect after Marriage

All of the boys anticipated economic problems after marriage, whether they came from families that were relatively well-off or if they came from very poor families. Those from poorer families were more concerned with providing basic necessities such as food, clothes and minimal housing. A major concern among all groups was finding a job. The girls, while mentioning economic problems, were more concerned with problems of family relationships. Their answers reflected the differences in socialization practices for village boys and girls. Boys were taught that economic matters were their responsibility, while girls were conditioned to be concerned about getting along with the families of their husbands. All of the girls anticipated problems in adjusting to their husbands and to the families of their husbands after marriage. Two boys (Cases 24 and 28), so concerned with the problems they may face with a family, said they did not want to marry.

> I do not want to get married. Marriage can damage
> the peace of life. There would be quarrels in
> the family. Also there are the general house-
> hold expenditures for the things one must buy
> for his wife and children. The education, clothing
> and many other things for children would cost
> too much. I don't want to know any more about
> family life. I am not going to get married.
> There is no need for it.

> Many repent after marriage. They cannot
> manage for themselves, how can they manage
> for two? You also lose your freedom. See,
> if you have a job in the city, if you are single,
> you can stay in a lodge and pay nominal rates.
> If you are married, you must have a room.
> Also brothers quarrel among themselves because
> of their wives. My father would spend so much
> money on my marriage. Why should I let him?

With sons, responsibility did not end with providing for their wives and their own children. It had been made clear to most of the boys as they were growing up that the importance of a son was to take care of his mother and father when they were older. This responsibility to the family of origin often also included brothers and sisters (Case 35).

> I will have to look after my family and provide
> support for their needs. I will also have to provide
> for my father and mother. I will have to take
> care of my younger brother and three younger
> sisters. All of these are a worry to me.

However, when there were no sons in the family, the daughter had the double worry, if not responsibility, of the welfare of those members of her family she left behind, as well as her obligation to the new family she joined (Case 39).

> Oh, yes! All the problems of my husband's family
> would become my problems. But I will always
> worry for my mother. Who is going to take care
> of her when I am away from my family? She
> is sick. If our income is not enough, how will
> I manage to support her?

The anxiety about going to the family of one's in-laws was well justified for the girls. There were many cases of harsh treatment and many more where the girl was sent home in disgrace because she did not perform as expected. This concern is expressed in the following comments of some of the girls (Cases 3, 4, and 8).

> I will have a problem with cooking and

household work. I will have to stay with strangers.
How will I feel with my new family? I think I
will be insecure.

You have to work for the family. If you have
sisters-in-law [husband's brother's wife], you
have to be good to them and have to adjust to
their ways.

Problems? Health would be my first problem.
I am not keeping well for almost the past four
years. I will have to work in spite of my bad
health. If my in-laws are very short-tempered,
they will become irritated about my illness.
They may not give me the medicine I need.

Control of Family Size as a Problem

Of the students, 16 (41 percent) commented on the
problem of limiting the number of children they had. With
economic responsibility, such comments were made largely by
the boys (Cases 34, 27, and 29).

The biggest problem I will face is earning enough
income in order to meet the needs of my wife
and children and my mother. This would be
a great problem if my family were larger.

There is the problem of meeting new responsibilities. I will be required to pay attention to
the needs of my children and to the health of my
wife. I think one of the problems, then, will
be to limit the size of my family. I would have
to know about the use of contraceptives. I know
care must be taken in using them or they will
not work. They must be used as directed by
the doctor.

After my marriage I am likely to face the problem
of how to control the size of my family. My
other friends also regard this as a problem because
they also come from large families where conditions

at home are difficult. All of this has an effect
on our thinking before we are married.

Those who did not mention family size as a problem were
then asked specifically whether controlling the size of their
family might be of concern. Only five students, all of them
girls, indicated they did not know whether controlling family size
would be a problem or not. The rest said they thought it might
be a problem.

One lower caste boy (Case 19), who was already married,
did not want to have children before he had finished his education.

I will tell you that this is a serious problem to
me and one to which I have given much thought.
I like the idea of family planning and I use the
condom method because I do not want children
until after I finish my education.

Another lower caste boy (Case 20) said it would be
important because he would have a smaller income than other
boys in the village.

Yes, controlling the size of my family will be
a problem. I am likely to get a smaller income
than other people. So I would like to have only
two children whether they are boys or girls.
If I had more than two children, it would really
be a hardship to feed them and take care of them
when they are sick.

High caste boys were also concerned about whether they
would be able to control the number of children they would have
but seemed to stress the importance of savings and adequate
space in the house rather than provision of basic needs of family
members (Cases 15 and 22).

This is a serious problem. I need to control
the size of my family so that I may have good
living. We would have peace. There would be
savings with a small family. My friends regard
overpopulation as a problem because they have
large families and they have divided a small

amount of land. Now it is impossible to make
a living on such a small portion of land.

Yes. Also my friends consider it a problem
because they realize that quarrels often take
place because of a large-sized family. I also
have friends who will not be in a position to
study further because of the sizes of their
families.

Cases 3, 5, and 11 are examples of the female students
who said they were uncertain about whether controlling family
size would be a problem.

No. The question of family size does not occur
to me.

I do not know. I have not given it any serious
thought.

I never think of the size of my family. It is not
good. Such thoughts might preoccupy the mind
and hamper studies.

Conclusion

In the comments made about their future, it was clear
that the students did not view married life as romantic. The
boys were concerned about the responsibility they would have
with a wife and family. The girls expressed fear of the
problems they would face in the home of their in-laws.

That life in the joint family can be difficult for the young
women has been illustrated by several studies of suicide in
Gujarat State (Government of Gujarat, 1966), which found that
the number of women committing suicide was twice that of the
men. Of those occurring between 1960 and 1964 for other than
physical or mental illness, 55 percent of the women were less
than 25 years of age and over 78 percent were less than 30. The
surveys found that almost 75 percent of suicides took place in
joint families.

Kapadia (1966:271), in a reference to the Gujarat study, states that what was found was true for Western India as a whole and probably for other parts of the country. He adds in explanation:

> The husband can tyrannize the wife in various
> ways and for various reasons. If he does not
> like her, or if he is attached to someone else,
> he may force her to end her life to make way
> for a second marriage. Dowry and related
> customs provide a good handle to the husband
> and his kin for humiliating, depressing and even
> beating the woman. Oppression of the daughter-
> in-law by her husband's kin is frequent and can
> be extremely vexatious. It is to be noted that
> the parents of the woman who suffers from physical
> and mental torture seldom stand by her or save
> her from persecution; considerations of social
> prestige keep them from interfering in the
> exercise of rights conferred by the ideal of
> patrivratya.[6] And neighbors share the same
> view and outwardly show similar indifference,
> even when they feel privately a sincere sympathy
> for the woman. The public attitude results in
> a peculiar situation. The sypathetic attitude of
> friends and neighbors toward the suffering woman
> is expressed in critical remarks against her
> husband and his family during her lifetime; but
> this mild social ostracism fails to bear any fruit
> and if her sufferings result in the woman's suicide,
> their feeling is one of relief rather than
> recrimination against the offender. If one of
> the woman's relatives should want to prosecute
> the husband or his parents for causing such a
> tragedy, he will be persuaded and pressed in
> all possible ways to give up the idea. Stranger
> still is the fact that someone else will soon be
> ready to give his daughter in marriage to the
> offender. The enormity of the injustice done
> to women by the social ideal is well understood
> and lamented; yet the force of tradition is so
> strong that the injustice finds no challengers.

While one might be inclined to assume that the customs which lie behind the high suicide rate are those of the lowest castes, the statistics show otherwise. The highest rates were found among the higher caste, Patidar, where the dowry system is practiced and, as we will see, only minor modifications have been made in the voice of either the boy or girl in the marriage arrangement.

Boys, then, regardless of family background, expressed concern over economic problems they would face after marriage. Girls on the other hand were most concerned with the adjustment they must make to the family of their husband. The economic concern of the boys was reflected in expressed concern over limiting family size. Girls on the other hand, with their concern over gaining an accepted position in the new family context, said little about limiting family size. Having children, particularly sons, would still be a prerequisite to status.

IX. Situational Variables
Regarding Fertility Control

The students generally said they wanted small families and were able to verbalize valid reasons for wanting to limit their family size. There is, however, a difference between stating a desire to limit family size before marriage and doing so later. One of the limitations on fertility control has been called the 'family action potentials' (Hill et al, 1959). This involves the relationships between husband and wife and their ability to communicate in a meaningful way. It may also involve the influence of the extended family from the standpoint of possible impediments to husband-wife communication and pressures placed upon the couple to conform to expectations of the extended family.

We will first look at how the students viewed the traditional methods of arranging marriage, willingness to live with in-laws and their views of the role of a son and wife (daughter-in-law). We will then ask if they believed a husband and wife should discuss such matters as family size and what influence they thought the extended family might have on their decision-making about family size.

The Arrangement of Marriage

It may be assumed that a variable in husband-wife communication in the early stages of marriage and their resultant ability to control their fertility may depend in part on how comfortable they feel with each other. In India, the fact that marriages traditionally are arranged by the parents and the couple have little voice in the matter often has resulted in an initial inability to talk together about family problems, particularly those related to the number of children they want and how they might control fertility. We were, therefore, interested in changes regarding these arrangements.

Eleven students, as explained by a high caste boy (Case 15) indicated that they might have a say in the selection of a mate. Most of these were high caste students. While their

109

parents might arrange a meeting between a prospective bride and groom, it appeared as if their own decision on the acceptability of the match could be a factor in whether or not the marriage would take place.

> The girl's parents approach our relative. My
> relatives would talk to my parents about the
> arrangement. If my mother and father say 'yes'
> to the match, then my relatives would arrange
> a meeting for me with the girl. If the girl and
> I want to marry, then a marriage is arranged.
> Usually a dowry is set by the boy's parents.

Five said, as stated in the remarks of a high caste boy (Case 22), a girl (Case 39), and a lower caste boy (Case 20), that the couples would be consulted, but that their opinions would carry no weight.

> Usually the girl's parents would talk to my
> parents. After the parents consulted their
> daughter, the proposal would be finalized. We
> are not able to talk with our match. Marriages
> are decided by our parents.

> Parents usually arrange the marriage. Both
> parties must meet at a third place. Usually the
> boy and girl and a friend of both families will
> sit together. The friend will then go away.
> Then the young couple will talk together and
> decide about each other. This is not the procedure
> for all couples. Sometimes the meeting between
> the young couple is just a farce. The parents
> have already decided. The children see each
> other, but they are obliged to approve their
> parents' choice.

> First a boy's or girl's parents decide about a
> bethrothal and then inform their child of their
> decision. A son or daughter always agrees
> because what his parents say must be respected.
> We are consulted, but our feeling has no weight.

The rest of the students said that either the boy or girl

were not consulted (Scheduled Caste male, Case 34) or did not
mention a consultation in their description of the marriage
arrangement (lower caste male, Case 30).

> The girl's parents come to see the boy. They
> talk to the boy's parents and see their son. If
> the boy's parents agree, the marriage for their
> son is fixed. The son would not be consulted.
> In our case, we have to give some amount of
> money to the girl's parents. After that, the
> marriage is settled.

> In my village and in my caste, marriages are
> settled by the parents. The girl's family first
> find out a good boy of a good family. Then the
> girl's parents go to his place and see him. The
> boy is accompanied by his relatives. The boy's
> parents then go to see the girl. If all is well,
> the marriage is arranged.

Place of Residence after Marriage
and Related Problems

The degree to which a young couple may control their own
fertility in part may relate to the influence of the extended family.
We, therefore, were interested in knowing if the students planned
to live with their parents and what advantages and disadvantages
they see in such an arrangement.

Thirty of the respondents said they would live with
parents or in-laws. One said he would if he and his wife could
get along with them. Another said he would if his parents wished.
Only two said they would not.

Twelve indicated they would live in the joint family
because it was a duty and a moral responsibility. Fourteen saw
it as an advantage because work would be shared. Nine
mentioned the shared fun of a joint family. Five said that
children would be better cared for. Four talked about the
guidance and security of the joint family. One saw the mother-
in- law as one who could intervene if there was a quarrel
between the husband and wife. Two saw pooled resources as an
advantage.

Fourteen students mentioned the disadvantages of living in the joint family. Ten said there would be more likelihood of quarrels over such things as who did each kind of work and one mentioned specifically that too much work would be expected of the daughter-in-law. One mentioned problems of adjustment and another that the house would be too crowded. One said that her work would increase and another that there would be less freedom. One mentioned greater dependency on parents. One said saving would be difficult and also noted that there would be less food.

From the comments, it was obvious that boys were more interested in living with their parents than girls were in living with in-laws.

The following comments of two high caste boys (Cases 16 and 24) indicate some of the reasons for living in the joint family.

Yes, I would like to live with my parents. This is one of my first obligations. This is useful to my whole family because I will be able to look after the family occupation which would mean less work for my father. I would do one-half the production. Next, I would augment my parents' income and therefore help take care of my brothers and sisters. If we don't reside with our parents after marriage, we would cause an emotional disturbance. For example, every parent's desire is that a son would help them in their old age. If all of a sudden a son lives separately, then because of his expenses he may not be able to pay his parents. Not only this, but who would look after the family property in old age? All of these factors have a great influence on my mind.

If I married, I would live with my parents. I think it is the duty of the son to live with his parents. They have faced many hard times in rearing me. We owe them something. We must serve them. There is nothing bad about living with one's parents.

The comments of two girls indicated their fear of the domination of the mother-in-law (Cases 1 and 8).

> Well, if there are quarrels between the daughter-in-law and the mother-in-law, and they cannot get along together, this is bad. If the husband's parents are not thoughtful people, you can be given more than your share of the work to do and they may expect you to do the work all by yourself.

> If my mother-in-law is wicked, it would be a hell of a problem for me. You have to go by the orders of your in-laws. I would have no freedom.

One girl, however, mentioned the role a mother-in-law could play in settling husband-wife quarrels (Case 9).

> It adds to the family income. You are free and not tied down to the home as there are others to look after matters. A husband and wife might quarrel due to their immaturity. A mother-in-law could intervene and help.

The increased possibility of fights was seen by some students as a major disadvantage of the joint family. This was expressed by a high caste male (Case 37) and two females (Cases 3 and 6).

> No. I would not live with my parents. My father believes that after marriage the young couple should live separately to avoid any quarrels in the family. If we live separately, good relations can be maintained. Love and affection would be the same as it was before marriage this way.

> The chances of conflict are more. The mother-in-law and daughter-in-law may feel jealous of each other in demanding the attention of the son.

> The chances of conflict are there. There is lack of freedom.

Characteristics of a Good Son

The respondents were asked how they viewed a son's obligations to his family. It was clear that the traditional view of the son as a major support to the extended family was held by all boys and girls. Typical comments are given by two high caste boys (Cases 25 and 28) and a Scheduled Caste boy (Case 35).

> I consider it my duty to help support my parents. This is whether or not I lived with them. I plan a separate household, however; I would like to live in the city.

> A son must look after his parents. He must keep them with him. He must provide all luxuries for his parents that he himself enjoys.

> Yes, the son has certain special things to do for the family. He must serve and support the parents in their old age. He should not harass them. He should ask for their advice on matters. He should not make it necessary for them to work. He should spend sparingly. He should lead the family to some higher state. He should raise the level of the family's income. He should make them more educated. He should raise their prestige in society.

The comments of two girls (Cases 8 and 39) made it clear that they also understood the duties of a son and would be likely to inculcate these same expectations in their own sons.

> A son must do as his parents direct him to do. He should provide food. He should bring cloth or any other family necessities. A son should have a good job and earn enough to fulfill the financial demands of the family. A son must look after his brothers and sisters when the father is gone. A son becomes the head of the family in such cases.

> If there is a son in the family, he should contribute to the family welfare. He should earn and serve

his parents. A son should not allow his father
to work in the fields after he is old. A good
son should do all the work. A son should
maintain the family. A son must also look after
his brothers and sisters. He must repay any
family debt if necessary.

Characteristics of a Good Wife

The categories used in describing the characteristics of
a good wife indicate that the students generally responded with
traditional expectations. It was evident that a majority still
believed the essential criterion of a good wife was her ability to
adjust to the joint family. Thirty-seven of the responses
mentioned ability to do household work and ten said the wife
should be expected to take a job outside the home to add to the
family income. A good wife is generally expected to obey her
husband and meet his sexual needs, and she should avoid
harming the family name by being familiar with other village
men. A wife should be good-looking. She must be dignified and
progressive. Education was mentioned by twelve students.

Some of the general expectations were expressed by one
high caste boy (Case 14) and two Scheduled Caste boys (Cases 35
and 36).

A good wife should have good conduct. She must
have good behavior and the ability to adopt my
family's customs. She must be able to care for
our children as they grow. She should have some
education. She must have good clothing when
she comes to me.

A good wife is one who would obey her husband
and respect his views. Most important, she should
have a good nature. She should also be attractive.
She should be educated to some extent, perhaps
ten years of education. She should not be a rigid
type of person.

I believe a good wife is one who would work for
the family. She would claim respect in society

by her good behavior. A good wife would be
one who respects my elders by covering her
head.

The girls themselves were well aware of the expectations
and seemed to accept them as indicated in the following
comments (Cases 1, 8, and 39).

A good wife must be a good housekeeper. She
must manage the home according to the family's
income. She should respect her in-laws, too.

A good wife would have to obey her mother-in-
law. She should not quarrel with her husband
or her in-laws. She would have to obey her
husband.

A woman who would make a good wife must be
well-educated and matured in her thinking. A
good wife must respect her husband's parents
and understand their difficulties. She must be
able to help solve their conflicts. A good wife
must not be a spendthrift. She should be helpful
to her husband.

The importance of being faithful to the husband and
meeting his sex needs was clear in two cases (high caste male,
Case 15, and lower caste male, Case 20).

A good wife is one who will serve her husband
and satisfy his sexual needs. It has happened
in our village that one married woman has not
satisfied her husband's sexual needs. This
woman denies her husband because she suspects
that he is having an extra-marital relationship.
This woman lives with his family, but she does
not allow him to have intercourse. This is what
other people say, too. I do know that this man
has a relationship with at least one person.
This person is married, and her husband does
not know about it. I think it may be free,
because this woman has good property from her
own home and her husband's property is good.

This well-off family resides in the middle of
the village.

A good wife must serve her husband. She must
be faithful to him. 'Faithful' means she will
not have extra-marital relationships. I know
that there are such relationships.

Expected Behavior of a Wife

To what extent did the students reject the traditional
subservient relationship between the new daughter-in-law and
her in-laws? One indication of a significant change in traditional
values might be an insistence on an increasing degree of equality.
However, when the students were asked how they expected wives
to behave with in-laws, little indication of change from tradition
was noted. Most of the students expected that a wife would be
obedient and respectful and behave in a way that would not harm
the status of the family.

It was interesting to note that there was no dissenting
voice among the girls regarding the traditional roles. In all
cases, they repeated the lessons they had learned regarding
proper behavior in the homes of their in-laws. Three comments
of the girls are indicative of what they all reported (Cases 2, 8,
and 12).

A girl must obey her in-laws. She should work
hand-in-hand with everyone. I will have to cook.
I will have to fetch water. I will serve them if
I am allowed to. I will respect and obey them.

I will have to cover my head for my father-in-
law. I will never be able to argue with him.
The same would be true for my husband's eldest
brother. I might not have to cover my head for
my mother-in-law, but I have to respect her
wishes. I might have to work even though I am
sick. This would happen only if my in-laws were
very mean. I will always have to obey and respect
my elders. I would have to look to the needs
of my sister-in-law.

I will be expected to respect my in-laws. I would
cook for them and clean. The main thing is that
I will be expected to obey my mother-in-law
and husband. I will have to love and serve the
younger ones in the family.

The following comments by four Scheduled Caste boys
make the expectations of a wife clear (Cases 31, 33, 34, and 35).

My wife will have to keep respect for my mother
and other brothers and sisters. She must respect
them so that quarrels do not arise. Otherwise
she would cause trouble to the mind. She must
adjust to the family in such a way as to diminish
all the disturbances. My wife must also assist
my mother. She must go to work in the fields
if it is required. I do not want my wife to have
to work in the fields, but if my mother works
and she sits quietly at home, it would not look
good. What would the people of the village think
of us ?

My wife must share the responsiblity of the family.
She should extend her help and cooperation in all
family activities to be undertaken. For example,
she must work with my brother's wife. She must
respect all family members, so that the family
remains unified forever.

My wife will be expected to work for the house
and for her children. She will be expected to
cover her head and obey my mother. She should
go to the fields and help with the tasks of farming.
She will respect my father by covering her head.
She will not speak directly to him. She may not
necessarily cover her head when my mother is
alone. She will always obey me.

She must put in her hand in the work of my parents.
She must respect all family members. She must
serve them. She should work in the kitchen and
adhere to my mother's will. She should not allow
my mother to work.

Two high caste boys (Cases 25 and 27) indicated the pressure on a girl to behave. Any real or imagined misconduct sexually was enough to be sent back to the parents' home in disgrace. If a girl did not work as expected or bear children, she might also face the possibility of being rejected. As a male student (Case 25) explained, since the boy had little to say in the selection of the girl, it may be of little concern to him what happens to her in or out of the household.

> There are cases of sexual dissatisfaction and the husband goes to another woman. It is easily justified for the husband to do this if the wife is not responsive or does not bear children. The husband does not have the major voice in the selection of the wife, so he feels he does not have much responsibility if the wife does not do as is customarily expected.

> In our caste, if a girl does not turn out well as a wife, the husband need not allow that girl to reside with him. This has happened. I know of a case where the son was married to a Patidar girl, but she was having relations with another man in the village. The husband soon found it out and sent her back to her parents.

Husband-Wife Discussion of Family Size

Traditionally in the joint family, early in marriage husbands and wives have little chance to talk together about family problems and the matter of family size may be regarded less as one of concern for the couple than that of the joint family. However, when the students were asked if a husband and wife should talk about the number of children they should have, 74 percent said 'yes.' Only one student said 'no.' Eight students (21 percent) said it should be discussed, but that the husband's choice should be final while one thought the wife's decision should be final.

Some students stressed the importance of discussing the number of children early in marriage. The comments of three girls, Cases 2, 7, and 11, are examples.

> They must talk about the size of the family they
> desire. They must do it before it is too late and
> the wife becomes stubborn in her views.

> Yes, a husband and wife should discuss what size
> family they desire early in their marriage.
> Both the husband and wife should jointly decide
> such a matter.

> I feel a husband and wife should discuss these
> points. This may be considered before it is too
> late. Both should have their say in this matter.

When asked who should decide about the size of the family,
most of the students thought the decision regarding family size
should be made jointly to avoid misunderstanding. Such
comments were common for all groups (high caste male, Case 38;
lower caste male, Case 18; Scheduled Caste male, Case 35).

> A husband and wife should talk about their family
> size. In the matter of deciding what the size
> should be, both husband and wife should have
> equal rights. This would avoid conflict.

> In matters of size of the family, both the husband
> and wife should decide, so as to avoid any
> quarrels later in life. If the decision is taken
> by the husband and if all the children die, then
> the wife might blame the husband forever.

> I think both the husband and wife should have
> their say regarding the size of the family. A
> husband should not decide himself. There are
> many reasons. Sometimes a woman dies in the
> delivery of a child. Women also lose their health.
> They cannot cook and work for a big family.
> There are also conflicts. So to avoid all of these
> problems, a wife must also have her voice in
> the decision.

Seven of the boys, while expressing the feeling that they
should consult their wives about the family size, believed that
they should have the final word (high caste male, Case 25;

Scheduled Caste male, Case 31).

> I would like to talk about the size of our family
> but my decision on the matter would be final
> because I am going to earn the income.

> A husband should decide about the size of the
> family because he is the person who is going to
> shoulder the entire responsibility of the family.

One of the girls, however, thought the final decision
should be that of the wife (Case 4).

> I feel a woman should make the final decision.
> She must decide because she loses her health and
> sometimes even her life by having many children.

A few of the boys and girls, according to tradition, first
expressed the feeling that the husband should have the final
decision and then decided it should be made jointly (high caste
male, Case 28; female, Case 39).

> I believe the size of the family should be
> discussed by both husband and wife. The husband
> should make the final decision concerning this
> as he has to bear the expenditure of having
> children. A wife should have her say too. She
> must make the children ideal. If there are too
> many children, she has to face their constant
> quarreling. She might lose her health with too
> many children. Yes, she should also have her
> say.

> I think the husband has the right to make the
> final decision. You see, a husband has to earn
> for the family. He has to pay all the bills. On
> the other hand, a mother should have her say.
> She has responsibilities, too. She has to look
> after their needs for the whole day. So I guess
> a wife should also have her say. Both a husband
> and wife should decide.

One of the girls (Case 8), while agreeing that the question of family size should be discussed, indicated the usual difficulty of husband-wife communication early in marriage.

> Yes, I think a husband and wife should talk about
> the problems of their family and that family size
> ought to be discussed. But not in the early days
> of marriage. I would feel shy to discuss those
> things when I was first married. But after I knew
> my husband well, I should talk to him. Any decision
> about the size of a family should be by mutual
> agreement. Both the husband wife have to bear
> the load of bringing up the children. Both have
> to decide how many children to have. The wife
> should have a special say because she loses her
> health with each delivery.

One boy (Scheduled Caste, Case 34) agreed that decisions should be made by the husband and wife but indicated the problems of husband-wife discussion in the joint family.

> A husband and wife must decide what size family
> they wish. However, it is difficult to discuss such
> matters in a joint family. Other members of
> the family would always be around us.

Influence of the Joint Family
in Determining Family Size

The students were asked the extent to which they believed their parents and in-laws might influence the number of children they would have, and if it would make a difference if they lived in the joint family or lived alone with their husband or wife. The question had quite different meanings for the girls and boys since, as we have seen, the boys often knew what their parents thought about family size. The girls, however, could only imagine the attitudes of their in-laws. With the strong conditioning of the girls for obedience, it was not surprising that most of them said that they would be influenced by the joint family. Some also indicated that they might have fewer children if they lived alone with their husband.

One girl (Case 1) said that it would be a two-step flow communication to her. She would do as her husband wished, but she had no way of judging how his parents would affect his decision.

> I cannot say about this. I will depend mostly on what my husband wants and I cannot say how they might influence him.

Three other girls indicated that they would by influenced by the joint family (Cases 5, 9, and 12).

> I don't know. I will consult a doctor. But also I will take advice from my mother-in-law.

> It is likely that I would have more children in the joint family because of my husband's mother.

> If I live in the joint family, I have to behave as a daughter-in-law and obey their wishes. If I lived separately, I would act according to my own wish.

One girl (Case 11) did not think it would make any difference if she lived alone with her husband or in the joint family in terms of her decision about family size. She said she would decide, but seemed somewhat uncertain.

> Well, I do not know. Living separately would not make any difference. If I let my mother-in-law interfere or respect her wishes, this would would be the same in both places. I feel, at least regarding the matter of children I want, that I will have my say.

Another girl (Case 2) admitted that her in-laws might have some influence, but she felt she could bring them around to her point of view if there was disagreement.

> To some extent my in-laws might influence the size of my family. But I will convince them somehow. If I lived separately, I would not have to convince anybody.

124

The girl who was ill much of the time (Case 8) seemed to feel that her life depended on having few children. As a result she must limit her family one way or another.

> Their ideas will not influence us. Their ideas
> would not determine the size of my family. I
> am not well now. I have no energy. So I will
> limit the family according to my will. I may
> do this openly or secretly somehow.

But another girl (Case 6) indicated the pressure she might encounter to have a son and was not sure she would be able to resist it.

> There would be no problem if I had sons to start
> with. I don't know if my mother-in-law's opinions
> would influence me if I had three daughters.

One female student (Case 39) said she would be firm about family planning, but only after having a traditionally acceptable three sons.

> I would like to have three to four children. I
> would like three sons and one daughter. I will
> practice family planning. I would do this even
> if my in-laws disapproved of my check on the
> family size. I will persuade and convince them.
> Of course, my ideas depend on the ideas of my
> husband's family too. But, regarding the size
> of my family, I will be firm.

Of the boys, only two (high caste, Cases 13 and 21) indicated that the joint family would determine their decision, possibly in the direction of having a larger family than they themselves might prefer.

> The joint family would have great influence on
> me. It is in the joint family that a son learns
> how to make his living in cooperation with others.

> If we stayed in the joint family, my mother's
> ideas on the size of the family would influence
> me. If we stayed in the joint family, we would

likely have more children. If we stayed all by
ourselves, we would have a very small family.

Four high caste students (Cases 16, 23, 25, and 29) made
it clear that they would determine their own family size.

When I have decided how many children I want,
the joint family would not interfere with my
decision.

Nobody can influence my idea once I decide about
the size of family I want to have.

I intend to live separately, and to take that
responsibility on my own.

No, of course one should follow traditions and
respect elders when it is their due. But in this
case, one's own decision should be final.

The other high caste boys repeated statements they had
made earlier regarding the influence they had already felt in
their family regarding the need for family size control. Four
students (Cases 15, 22, 26, and 27) reported that their parents
had already advised them to have small families.

I believe that my parents' advice about having
a small family has already made me think about
the problem. Otherwise I would have no idea
about it. I have known this since I was in the
8th Standard.

The joint family has influenced by thinking. My
father is a doctor so I know something about
the why and how of family planning.

They will influence us greatly. They have already
influenced my wife by telling her that a small
family is good.

My father has had much influence on my decision
to have a small family. But I have also thought
about it, and read a book on family planning.

Four other high caste boys (Cases 14, 27, 37, and 38) also indicated the direct influence of the family regarding the desirability of family size control.

My parents have already had a small family and like it. This has influenced me. We are only two brothers and one sister and we can maintain ourselves very well with this small number.

No, my father and I agree that a small family is best.

It is the present situation in my family that has affected my thinking regarding a small family.

My mother's experience when her twins died during delivery and when her health became weak has really influenced me. The condition of my home has also made me think about a small family.

Of the boys from lower caste and community backgrounds, all either would resist any family pressure to have more children than they wished or believed that they had already been influenced by their family to limit family size.

Four boys (Cases 19, 30, 34, and 36) indicated that they would make their own decisions regarding family size.

I have firmly decided that I shall have two children and no more. Whether I live with the family or alone, it makes no difference. But I intend to live separately from my family. That has been decided.

No, I think I will respect their authority in many ways, but will go by my decision in matters of the size of the family.

An individual must decide if he wants a small family or not. It is not the joint family which matters in such a decision. Of course, the circumstances of joint household plays an important role.

Yes, my parents' ideas could influence me to
some extent. But as far as the size of my family
is concerned, I will go by my decision. In this
case it doesn't matter whether I live alone or with
my parents.

One boy (Case 35) said that although he would not ignore
his parents, he would do the best he could to have them see his
point of view.

Yes, I believe such moments do come in life.
They would help when you have to choose between
two things of the same importance. I don't think
I would betray or insult them. I will try to convince
them about my preferences. In the end I would
not suffer the way they did. I will try my best
to limit the size of my family.

With the rest of the lower caste and community boys,
(Cases 17, 18, 20, 29, 31, 32, and 33), no disagreement with
parents was indicated. Again, as we have seen previously,
parental influence and family experiences had been a major factor
in determining their desire for family size control.

It is the family circumstances that I now
experience such as our low income and large
family, which have led me to think about the
small size of a family that is needed.

I don't think family influences the idea about
size. Looking to present circumstances like
poverty, food shortage, we must think about what
size of family we can afford. It would pay the
family and the nation too. A family can be happy
within a limited income if the size of it is small.
If the population is reduced, shortages can easily
be avoided.

My parents' influence will be great. My father
talks about the condition of our family. When
I see him working so hard, I feel I must have
a small family.

My parents have already influenced my
thinking about a small family. They always
talk about the advantages of having a small
family. With a small family, you can avoid
most of the trouble.

We will have a small family. Their talk has
already influenced our attitude.

My family has already influenced my thinking.
My family is passing through such a stage when
the size of the family has to be considered.

It is not only my parents that will influence the
number of children we will have. That is always
there. Reading newspapers, the prevailing
situations at other homes — these too change
one's thinking about the size of the family.

Conclusion

Between desired family size, on the one hand, and the
control of fertility, on the other, are not only available methods
of control but a set of situation variables which permit the
effective use of such methods.

One is the degree to which the couple may be able to
communicate with each other. The traditional arranged
marriage and the structure of the joint family has not facilitated
husband-wife communication. What change, then, did we find
in the traditional pattern?

Of the students, 23 indicated that the traditional pattern
of not consulting them regarding their marriage would be
followed. Five said that they might be consulted but that they did
not expect any objection on their part to the person selected for
them would make any difference. However, 11 students said they
did expect to be consulted and the marriage would be arranged
only if they agreed to marry the boy or girl. The data indicate
movement in some families from completely ignoring the wishes
and feelings of the boy and girl to at least consulting them. This
was most evident among the higher caste students.

Only two students of the 34 who answered a question
regarding place of residence after marriage said they would not
live in the joint family. Many of the students mentioned the
disadvantages of living in the joint family but it was clear that
they saw it as a duty and moral responsibility.

All of the students accepted the traditional role of the son
and his oblication to the joint family. For the wife, again the
traditional role of subservience was accepted with little
indication of an increasing demand for equality, even among the
girls.

In spite of the seeming belief in and acceptance of
traditional roles, most of the students believed that husbands and
wives should discuss the number of children they want, although
eight of the students believed that, even though discussed, the
decision of the husband should be final. When asked directly
about the possible influence of the joint family in determining
family size, most of the girls said they would be influenced and it
would probably mean having more children than they might have
if they lived alone with their husband. The boys, who knew their
own family situation, seemed to feel that they would be able to
determine the number of children they wanted without parental
interference. Only two boys said that the joint family would
determine their decision.

The analysis of the data seem to indicate that, although
the boys and girls remained traditional in their acceptance of sex
roles, most thought they would be able to talk to their husband or
wife about the number of children they should have and the boys,
at least, believed they would be able to make their own decision
without parental interference. This confidence on the part of the
boys seemed to be due, in part, to the fact that they believed
their parents thought as they did about the proper number of
children to have, and, as a result, there would be no conflict.

Assuming that desired family size has decreased
somewhat for these young people and that they will be able to
make decisions within the joint family, how will they then control
their fertility? The next section will examine their knowledge of
reproduction and methods to prevent conception.

X. Knowledge of Reproduction, Methods to
Prevent Conception and Need for More Information

Many of the students, particularly the girls, would soon
be married. If, as many indicated, they wished to prevent
conception for a few years, to space their children, and to
terminate fertility after they have the number of children
desired, it would require some knowledge of reproduction and
contraceptive methods. We, therefore, tried to determine what
the students knew concerning how conception took place and how
it might be prevented. We also asked if they felt that the
knowledge they had was adequate and if they would like more
information.

Knowledge of Conception

When the students were asked how conception takes place,
all of the boys seemed aware that intercourse was required.
However, it was not clear in the translation how much of the
details of reproduction were actually understood. The comments
of Cases 17, 35, and 36 were typical.

Usually a husband and wife have intercourse.
During this, at the end, two seeds, one male
and one female, unite. This grows for nine
months and then a child is born.

A child is conceived by the touch or contact of
a man and a woman. A man comes in contact
with a woman and semen is stored in the abdomen
of the woman. After nine months, a boy or girl
is born. If the strength of the semen of the man
is greater than that of the woman, the baby is
a boy. If the semen of the woman is stronger,
then it is a girl.

A child takes ten months to be born. God's
blessings are not all there is to it. A girl has
to be with her husband. A pregnant lady has a
child in her womb. She should be taken care of.

131

She must have good food. She should be taken
to a doctor periodically. The seed of a man and
the seed of a woman unite to give rise to a child
in the womb of a mother. After some months
the child is born.

The girls generally said they could not describe the
process of conception, as with Cases 8 and 9.

A child is conceived by the very close contact
of a man and a woman. I know what happens but
I cannot describe it. It is physical. Just as in
flowers, the male seeds go to the female seeds
and a child is conceived.

I do not know much about childbirth. It takes
nine to ten months. One has to get married.
Husband and wife together have to do something
for conception. A mother needs extra care and
attention and rest during pregnancy.

One girl (Case 4) added the fear common to village
parents and girls that a girl might become pregnant before
marriage.

I do not have any idea about how conception takes
place. I know that mothers worry about their
grown-up girls. Mothers tell us that roaming
about alone is dangerous. Some male might
take advantage of a girl who is alone. He might
misbehave. The girl might conceive. I cannot
express it, but I know what happens. If someone
came with a bad look in his eyes, a girl should
run away. Otherwise unwanted things might
happen. She might conceive.

Knowledge of Birth Control

When the students were asked if they knew of ways to keep
from having a baby, they were all able to mention one or more
methods. However, the comments did not indicate they knew
much about them. The comments of two boys are examples

(Cases 14 and 18).

> Operations are the best ways to limit the size
> of a family. I don't know anything about other
> methods of family control. I know that there is
> such a thing as a loop and condom.

> Contraceptives and operations are ways to limit
> the size of the family. I know about the loop and
> diaphragm, but I have not seen them.

Neither were the girls well informed as indicated by the comments of Cases 9, 12, and 39.

> I know only the name of loop and operation.
> I do not know the details.

> Children can be kept away by family planning.
> There are operations for males and females.
> Loops are in women. Celibacy is a way. Jelly
> and other drugs are available. I do not know
> about others, but harmful drugs like quinine
> and some home-made medicine can produce
> abortion.

> An operation for the woman is the surest way
> to prevent the birth of children. The doctor
> would remove the bag. The tube is also sealed
> by sutures. Another method is to observe
> celibacy. Loop insertion is a popular thing for
> ladies. I have heard them talk about the loop
> on the train. I don't know what men can do for
> family planning. Men can have an operation,
> but I don't know anything about the details.

Need for Information about Family Planning

When the students were asked if they felt a need for information about family planning, 33 of the 39 said they would like to know more about it. Two girls (Cases 8 and 11) illustrate the comments of some of the six students who did not think such information was needed at their age.

134

>   I do not think persons of my age should be
>   concerned about it. This is no time to think
>   about the size of the family. We can think about
>   it when the right time comes. If we think about
>   it now then we may not be able to concentrate
>   on anything else.

>   No, it would not be good. One might become
>   preoccupied with this. It might hamper our
>   studies.

Only one boy (Case 19) stated that he already knew enough about family planning.

>   No, I don't think I need to learn about it. I
>   already know what to do. I use condoms. I
>   went to see the family planning clinic right after
>   I was married. They told me what I needed to
>   know.

The comments from most of the students, however, as with Case 26, indicated that they would be interested in having more information than they had.

>   I think it is necessary to learn more about the
>   problems of family life because I am certain
>   I do not know many things about it. I tried very
>   hard after I was married to learn more about
>   family planning so that I would know about it
>   in detail. I do not know everything.

Conclusion

The boys were clearly aware that sexual intercourse was required for conception to take place. Interviews with older men in Rajpur village indicate that village boys often have their first sexual experience long before the average age of the students interviewed. Sex was a frequent topic of conversation among the boys and, in addition to those who were already married, many of the others had already had intercourse. They also understood the relationship between intercourse and pregnancy.

While it was acceptable for boys to talk about sex in their groups, and premarital sexual relations were usually overlooked, girls were not expected to discuss such things and there was a strong taboo against any sort of premarital association with a boy. Neither did the mothers discuss sex with their daughters. What information the daughters got before marriage they usually received from a recently married friend. Girls, therefore, were generally less well informed than boys.

The students knew little more than the names of various methods of fertility control. Most of them had heard of the IUD and sterilization. However, the IUD was not acceptable because of feared side effects and young couples would not have an operation. They gave little evidence of knowing of methods which might be available to them early in marriage. Two students mentioned the diaphragm; one, coitus interruptus; and six, celibacy. No one mentioned the rhythm method, although some villagers in the area did claim to use it. The condom, however, was mentioned by ten students and seemed to be the best method available for the youth in spite of its frequent rejection as something used only with prostitutes.

In general, then, knowledge of reproduction and contraception was minimal for effective fertility control and the students seemed aware of the fact. Thirty-three students said they would like to have more information than they had.

The next section considers how such information may be given to the village youth.

XI.   Teaching Reproduction and
Family Planning in the Village School

Since we were interested in possible problems in teaching
reproduction and family planning in the school, we asked the
students what support the villagers gave to the government family
planning program. We then asked about how their parents might
react to teaching reproduction and family planning in the schools
and what they themselves thought about it. Finally, we asked
how they thought the subject should be taught.

Village Support for Family Planning

All but four students (90 percent) indicated that some
villagers were in favor of family planning and some were not.
The degree of believed opposition varied from a feeling that most
of the villagers opposed the program to the belief that most were
supportive of it.

A few said that the concept of family planning itself was
objected to as in the case of a lower caste male (Case 18).

Some people in the village talk against the program
because they believe it is a sin to keep away a
baby.

Some said rejection came largely from the elderly and the
more orthodox as indicated by two girls (Cases 5 and 10).

Some people do benefit by the family planning
program. But the old people take it as unnatural.

People like it. The very orthodox people, however,
do not approve of it.

Most comments indicated that the objections to the
program were on a pragmatic basis rather than moral or
religious. As indicated by one girl (Case 39), the concern had
to do largely with the fear of the effect of available methods on
health and the concern that if an operation was resorted to, the

137

children might die and one could not have any more.

> You see, you cannot really say what people feel.
> Some, who realize the importance of a small
> family, like it. Some abhor family planning
> because they know of cases where the loop has
> failed. Ben [sister] , it suits some to have the
> loop, but not others. With the operation some
> argue that if they have two daughters and one
> son, and if the son dies, then it is not possible
> for the woman to conceive again. This means
> your family ends with you.

One high caste boy (Case 16) said that dissatisfaction with
the program had to do with quality of service at the medical
center.

> People don't like the family planning program
> because the medical center does not take proper
> care of them in terms of [follow up] treatment.
> My neighbor had a loop inserted. It caused heavy
> bleeding. So her health was affected. Besides
> this, she conceived even though the loop was
> inserted.

Others said that acceptance of the program had to do with
educational level as stated by a girl (Case 4) and a lower caste
boy (Case 20).

> There are some who like it. But there are also
> some who do not believe in such things. They
> are illiterate so they may not like it. Some feel
> the operation harms the health of the women.

> Those who are educated say family planning has
> a good program because happiness in a family
> goes side-by-side with controlling its size.
> But most people believe family planning is not
> a good program. They believe there will be no
> one to support them in old age if the family is
> too small. Many sons mean more income.

Parental Acceptance of Teaching Reproduction and Family Planning in the Schools

The students were divided on what they thought the attitude of their parents might be to teaching reproduction and family planning in the schools. Half of the students indicated parental approval but others did not know what their parents might think.

One high caste boy (Case 25) thought parents in the village were too conservative to permit it, but that it might be taught in the city.

> I think it would be good but I think in this village, where everything is done according to custom and tradition, there would be much resistance to introducing the subject into the schools. The teaching of family life would be possible in the city, but not here.

However, the girl whose father was a doctor (Case 12) not only said such a program would be acceptable to him, but that he would be willing to help in instruction.

> Yes, my father would like it. He could come and teach it also.

The belief that parents would accept family planning teaching was expressed by some members of all groups among the boys. The following comments of Cases 17, 18, 27, and 30 are illustrative.

> I don't believe my parents or other family members members would object to such classes.

> I think no one would object to it because it would be good to plan the family's life before one is married.

> I don't know about other parents, but mine would welcome teaching about family planning since they look forward to adjusting to a modern atmosphere.

My father would like it. I think he realizes the
importance of a small family.

Two students, one female (Case 4) and one male (Case 21)
indicated it would be helpful to include parents in the planning of
such programs. They seemed to feel that if the program were
explained, their parents would not object to having the subject
taught in school.

I think my parents would welcome this effort
if they are taken into confidence in a proper
way.

If parents are taken into confidence then they
might agree. Otherwise in the village, they
may oppose teaching about family planning.

Students' Attitudes Regarding the Teaching
of Reproduction and Family Planning

While most students reported they would like to have
reproduction and family planning taught in the school, most of
them indicated it would be a difficult subject for teachers to
handle. Three students (Cases 22, 27, and 37) thought such
information might be misused and should not be taught.

It is not good to teach about this thing in the
school. It might lead to the misuse of contraceptives. Students are not that mature. Of
course learning about family planning would
have a good effect in the future, but the evils
misuse would produce would last for 100 years
to come.

I do not think family planning should be taught.
I say this because many students, especially
those of lower castes with very immature minds,
would probably misuse the information. I know
that low caste boys and girls have intercourse
when they are coming back from the fields at
night. I have actually seen this happen.

I do not think that education in school about family
planning would be beneficial. This may lead to
misuse because during this age, youth are at
a point when they are likely to commit anti-social
acts. I think that family planning centers or some
other places can guide married couples in this
regard.

Two boys, one lower caste (Case 18) and one Scheduled
Caste (Case 33) said they would like to have the subject taught in
school, but they suggested that if that were not possible, youth
might get the necessary information from a family planning
clinic.

If the school takes up the program it would be
helpful, particularly knowing about contraceptives.
To my mind, the family planning centers would
be important if people objected that the school
was not the place to talk about it. Elder people
might think that the child is likely to move toward
misuse of contraceptives if he is taught about
it.

I think it is not good to teach about family planning
to students in school. We have orthodox parents.
Usually village people are orthodox. They live
by custom and traditions. So they would not send
their children to school if they taught about family
planning. The result, instead of increasing the
educational level of the people, would be to
diminish it. If you ask me about my personal
opinion, I would prefer that the school teach about
family planning, but if others oppose it we should
learn about it from the family planning centers.
This would really be the best way.

A Scheduled Caste boy (Case 35) said he would like such
information, but suggested that it would be best to offer a
special course on it to SSC students in the vacation period.

I would welcome the information. I think it is
necessary to teach it in school; but not now. I
It should be introduced after SSC during the

vacation so that it does not prove a distraction
from the SSC subjects. If it has to be taught with
other subjects, it should be taught from the 8th
Standard so that students get a proper knowledge
by the time they are ready to leave school. To
avoid any embarrassment, there should be only
boys in the class. Perhaps 20 to 25 students
would be the best but the number of students or
their caste is no point to consider. The teacher
should be a male so that the boys could feel at
ease in asking questions.

A girl (Case 10) thought the subject should be optional.

All students should not be made to study about
family planning. Only those who would like to
should be made to study it.

Although it was obvious that a major objection to teaching
reproduction and family planning, both on the part of the students
as well as the villagers, was the possiblity of misuse of the
information, several students, as with one high caste boy (Case
14), believed it might prevent premarital sexual activity.

Family planning should be taught in SSC so that
it will have a maturing effect on the students'
minds. This would make them think in the proper
way about sex. In our village some students go
to the fields or a temple for sexual intercourse.
This happens during religious festivals in Por
village.

One high caste boy (Case 13) and a lower caste boy (Case
19) did believe it should be given before the SSC level.

One must learn about sex education and contraceptives. This would prevent one from committing
a bad act in society such as having illegal intercourse. I think if education in family planning
started from the 8th Standard then it would prevent
one from committing anti-social activities.
During the 8th Standard one of my classmates
went to one of the school girl's house.

This girl was alone and he took intercourse by
force. The girl had to suffer much.

I think it is important to teach about it at least
beginning with the 8th Standard. I will tell you
why. In our village there was a boy studying in
the 9th Standard and he fell in love with a Patidar
girl who had been to school only to the 7th Standard.
She was sixteen years old. Well, she got pregnant
and would not tell the parents who the boy was.
The parents managed to get an abortion for her
and finally got her married. If she had learned
about these things, and the boy also, they might
not have done these things and she could have
been saved so much shame, pain and embarrassment.

Another high caste boy (Case 15), who thought
reproduction and family planning should be taught from 9th
Standard, pointed out that it would then tie in with the teaching of
physiology which was given at that level.

It should be started from the 9th Standard.
During this time, a student already learns about
the physiology of man and woman.

A Scheduled Caste boy (Case 32) thought it could be
started even earlier and tie in with the study of reproduction in
plants and animals in the 8th standard.

This subject of sex, its use, and how one should
think about family planning, should be taught
in school. The why and how of family planning
should be taught in school. Teaching about family
planning can be started from the 8th Standard.
During this year we also learn about fertilization
in flowers. So family planning subjects could be
added.

Methods of Teaching
Reproduction and Family Planning

There was one area of complete agreement. Both boys and girls believed that the subject should be taught separately. This was made clear by the following examples from a high caste boy (Case 16), a lower caste boy (Case 20) and a Scheduled Caste boy (Case 34).

> Classes should be separate to avoid shame.
> A male teacher would be more suited to class
> discussion with boys. We would be able to talk
> to him without hesitation.

> If the lessons were taught to boys and girls
> separately, this would help a lot because girls
> feel shy. If the teacher is a man, then he would
> be able to speak without omitting certain things.

> Boys should be separated from girls to avoid
> shame. It would not be possible to talk about
> this topic when boys and girls do not even talk
> to each other at other times. I would prefer
> to be taught by a male teacher so that if we
> wanted to ask some questions, we would not
> hesitate.

Three girls (Cases 3, 4, and 8) expressed the feelings typical of the females.

> It should be taught to girls alone. Small groups
> are best and I would prefer a lady teacher.

> The class should be for girls only. I would not
> matter what size, but it would be necessary to
> have a lady teacher.

> Classes should contain only girls. It could not
> be a man teaching.

In terms of the method of presentation, 19 students expressed a preference for the lecture method with some reading but did not mention discussion. As examples, the statements of a lower caste boy (Case 19), one from a higher caste (Case 27) and a Scheduled Caste boy (Case 34) are given.

> I think there should be lectures and reading
> material. Then tests could be given to determine
> how much was learned.

> Lectures would be best but the language should
> be clear and understandable. Afterwards they
> could recommend books to the students so they
> could get more information.

> Lecturing would be best because that is the way
> all other subjects are taught. Books should be
> provided so we could understand the topic fully.

One Scheduled Caste boy (Case 31), however, did not think books would be too useful.

> Lectures would be the best way to teach about
> family planning. Reading would be too taxing.

On the other hand, a high caste boy (Case 24) thought that books alone would be best.

> Books would be the best method of teaching so
> that no talk would be necessary.

The students specifically recommended discussion, usually along with lectures and reading. These students, as in the case of two high caste boys (Case 2 and Case 23), thought discussion would be helpful in developing further understanding of the subject.

> First, give books to the students to read. Then
> lecture and allow them to conduct discussion.
> Books would give ideas and discussion could
> clarify the ideas.

> The best way to teach about family planning would
> be to have teachers talk to us and give us books.
> Then we should discuss our understanding. We
> would have the advantage of knowing what doubts

other students have that we might not have
realized.

While many of the girls were interested in group
discussion with other girls, three (Case 8, for example) said
they would be more comfortable with reading assignments and
individual conferences.

Books should be used so you would not feel shy.
I feel that books should be given and then
individual conferences could be arranged to solve
difficulties.

Conclusion

The issue of what should be included in population
education from the standpoint of sex education has been debated
in India at some length (Kuppuswamy et al, 1971). Some have
stressed the importance of sex education while others have said
it should not be included in population education. Our data would
indicate that caution is necessary. We have seen that the
secondary schools were instituted and controlled by the village
leadership and an important reason for building such schools was
to protect the virginity of higher caste girls. To the extent that
village leaders may associate lack of knowledge regarding
matters of sex with virginity, they may be opposed to having sex
education in their schools. However, this does not indicate the
area should be ignored. Students reported little adult opposition,
on moral and religious grounds, to the family planning program,
indicating that most people objected to it on the basis that the
methods were not adequate. This finding agrees with other
studies in the area (Anker, 1973). About half the students
believed that reproduction and family planning might be taught in
the school, and two students recommended parental involvement
as a way to decrease critical parental comment.

A few students said they, themselves, believed
reproduction and family planning should not be taught because the
information might be misused. Others believed that providing
sex education would prevent premarital intercourse and it was
clear that a majority were in favor of having such information
provided. However, most of the students also confirmed

discussions with the teachers that indicated it is a subject that would be difficult to teach and discuss. The students made a number of suggestions such as a special course for students during the vacation period or that the topic be made optional. One student thought it could be taught through the family planning clinic or that clinic personnel might be responsible for the subject in the classroom.

If the subject was to be taught in school, the students agreed that boys and girls should not be in the same room. The majority preferred to have lectures given, although some wanted group discussion. Some of the girls, however, were so shy about the subject that they suggested only reading assignments and then individual discussion with the teacher.

The issue of what should be taught in the way of reproduction and family planning in village schools needs careful investigation but it would seem programs are possible. To begin with, human reproduction is already in the curriculum in secondary schools in the region. The teaching of it needs only to be improved and that would seem to be the first minimal step. Whatever else might be done would depend on what can be made acceptable to a particular community.

Clearly however, there is a need for sex, reproductive, and family planning education. The question is not if it should be taught to those about to marry, but how it can be done most effectively. Perhaps the most effective program the government can undertake is assisting the next generation to have the number of children they want. To ignore them until they have three or four children not only creates problems for young people but is a serious handicap to the achievement of the goals of the family planning program.

Summary and Conclusion

The 1971 census estimates the population of India at 548 million (Government of India, 1971, Table 1). The projection for the future are staggering. For the population of India to eventually level off at one billion people, the birthrate will have to be cut in half by 1985. This would mean that married couples would have to have, on the average, not more than 2. 4 children by that date (Population Reference Bureau, 1970).

In recognition of the problem, by the middle sixties, the Indian Government had begun the development of an extensive nation-wide family planning program. By the end of the sixties, a family planning center was attached to each of the 25,000 centers and sub-centers whose personnel were serving an increasing number of the nation's more than 500,000 villages (Chandrasekhar, 1968) and the total program employed over 100,000 persons (Soni, 1971).

Repeated studies in India have indicated that though an increasing number of people knew about the various methods of family planning offered by the government, only a small percentage of eligible couples used them. In addition, follow-up studies indicated a high discontinuation rate for such contra- ceptive methods as the IUD and condom. The national program has, therefore, concentrated on surgical sterilization in recent years. While these programs have been successful in bringing in large numbers of people, using cash payments as incentives, the average number of children they had at the time of steriliza- tion ranged between four and five. In addition, it was clear that few couples had been willing to terminate their fertility until they had several sons.

Critical comments of the Indian family planning program and those foreign agencies which assisted have been made with increasing frequency. Critics say that the family planning programs in India have failed because Indian villagers have had more to gain by having large families than by controlling their fertility (see Freedman and Berelson, 1976, for a recent examination of this issue). Certainly for the older generation in the region where we conducted our study, as well as for most of

149

India, the record clearly showed little demonstrated results in spite of the massive effort expended.

Our focus, however, was on the younger generation. The experiences of the youth we studied had been quite different than those of their parents. The problem of population pressure was a relatively new one and it takes time for the individual to personalize the meaning of change in any society. Widespread death from famine and plague occurred relatively recently in the area. In Gujarat, from 1896, and off and on for well over a decade, famine and the plague took large numbers of lives (Government of Baroda, 1911).

The 1931 census reported the population of the smaller area, in which the village studied was located, dropped from 90,641 to 69,221 between 1891 and 1901. By 1931, three decades later, the population was still under that of 1891 (Government of Baroda, 1931). The parents of some students grew up hearing stories of how the majority of members of some village families had died during this period. When the senior author first began work in this area in 1961, he talked to two old men who said they were old enough to remember the anxiety of the the time.

The young people in the sample, though, had grown up during a period of increasing crowding in the limited space available in the village. A question asked as villagers sat talking in front of their houses, observing the activity on the street, was, 'How are there so many children now?' In spite of villagers' continued fear that children might die, they were also aware that a great many lived. There was an increasing awareness that perhaps many more were living than were required.

In the present monograph, we have reported on the sources of information the students received from the mass media, and from the government family planning program, about population as a problem. In addition, we have paid particular attention to the informal learning that had taken place as a result of living from day to day with the problems faced by the village in general but particularly by those faced by the families of the youth. This seemed to be learning of most meaningful kind. The students did learn from the mass media. Far more important were the economic problems faced by many of the village families and the awareness of parents that large families were a complicating variable. We found that this increasing awareness was often communicated by parents to their children.

The major motivation for change did not seem to come, as it has been claimed in the West, because of a breakdown in the extended family, with youth moving out on their own. As we see it, the extended family remained very much intact. A major reason was that the rewards and punishments of the social system were still mainly through caste and the extended family, and these would seem to remain as long as no institutional framework replaced them. Industrialization in the West apparently moved rapidly enough with the increase in population to provide jobs for most youth who wished to leave the traditional home and the restraints of the extended family. In addition, change took place slowly enough so that new social mechanisms were developed in urban areas to meet such needs as mate selection. In India, the population growth occurred at a much more rapid rate. Industrialization had not been able to develop apace and provide employment for all who sought it. As a result, youth continued to depend on the extended family, not only for the increasing years of education required to qualify for jobs, but for family influence to obtain jobs, once they were qualified. In addition, they continued to be dependent on the extended family for marriage arrangements for there was hardly the beginning of a system of courtship to replace it. The students themselves remained traditional in their attitudes toward their obligations to the extended family and its return obligations to them. Socialization practices had not changed significantly and neither had basic values of having children and their role expectations. Essentially, children were still needed for the same reasons they had always been needed. What had happened was that more children were living than the number which was required under current economic conditions and these additional children were beginning to cause instability in the social structure.

The desire to have smaller families was not necessarily associated with a higher standard of living. The majority of students in this sample were from high caste families which were generally represented by students in the higher secondary schools of the area. For some of their families, particularly those having large landholdings, wealth was increasing. But some of these students represented lower caste and/or low

status families and, although they were the minority in the
school, families of these groups made up the large majority of
the population in the area.

Many villagers claimed that things were getting worse
economically than they had been in the past. At a time of rising
prices for essential items such as food, clothing, and housing,
and the desire for the increasing quantity of consumer goods,
there were fewer available jobs. The larger number of
unemployed and underemployed persons created a reservoir of
manpower willing to work, often for lower wages than in the past.
Employers were also in a position to increase educational
requirements for all types of jobs and occupational levels.
While this had the advantage of raising the general educational
level of the population, it also meant that poor families had to
spend a greater percentage of family income on the education of
their sons. It meant that to make a son economically profitable
a greater investment was required than in the past, and
increasingly, even with this greater investment, there was no
longer assurance that sons could be profitably employed.
McNamara (1971) has confirmed this general trend in the
developing countries in his Annual Report of the World Bank. He
reported that in 75 developing countries making up 96 percent of
the world's population, production and income had grown at an
average annual rate of more than 5.5 percent over the past ten
years. However, in spite of the average increase in higher
incomes and production, poverty in the world was increasing.
Statistics, he said, concealed the seriousness of the underlying
economic and social problems such as unequal distribution of
income and excessive levels of unemployment. This uneven
distribution of wealth was clearly evident in the families of the
students and it was the high castes with the largest incomes that
appeared to be least concerned about family limitation. For
these families at least, there is no evidence to support the
position that interest in family planning will come about only as
a result of raising economic status. Nor may additional
education make significant short-run differences.

The fathers of the students from high caste families with
no economic problems had an average of eight years of schooling.
In high caste families with economic problems the father had
less than five years of schooling. In the lower caste and
community families, the fathers had virtually no education.

However, from what we know of the area, it is not education that
has brought about an increase in economic status. Rather those
who already had high economic status have been responsible for
the building of secondary schools in the area. The resulting
education has, however, made it possible for boys from high
caste families to take jobs available to them because of caste
connections. The education of village girls was associated
largely with the need to increase their value in bartering in the
marriage market.

Some of the lower caste and community boys get better
jobs than they would have if they had not attended secondary
school. However, with few jobs available, these tended to go to
those who held the advantage in terms of the social and economic
structure of the region. The possibility, then, of education paying
off for the poor was severely limited. The situation was not
dissimilar to that described by Guthrie (1971:120) in regard to
another country:

> It is commonly assumed that achieving a high
> percentage of literacy and raising the education
> level of the population will hasten the other
> processes of modernization. However, it seems
> safe to say that increasing levels of education
> may follow rather than precede modernization,
> as was the case in Europe, and that a relatively
> high level of education can be achieved without
> a corresponding improvement in the standard
> of living, as is the case in the Philippines.

Obviously a decline in fertility rates would make a
significant contribution to the economic situation and since at
least some of the villagers were interested in limiting family
size, continued efforts on the part of the government,
particularly contraceptive education for youth, would seem to be
one practical way to improve the conditions of the poor.

In general, however, as we have pointed out, although the
students indicated a desire for relatively small families, there
was also evidence of acceptance of traditional roles associated
with high fertility. This fact may be expected to slow the decline
of fertility in the area.

Notes

1. The name of the village is fictitious.

2. One rupee was equal to about ten U.S. cents on the free market. Reported income is a rough estimate.

3. The percentage of students from the Scheduled Castes is in part accounted for by the fact that the government provides financial aid for students for both those from former 'untouchable' groups and from tribal groups. This support includes payment of dormitory or housing fees while attending secondary school. It should be pointed out that while support is offered to both Scheduled Castes and Tribes, it is used to a greater extent by Scheduled Castes. To what extent such aid might be used by middle and lower caste Hindus who are often in no better economic positions than those in the Scheduled Castes is unknown.

4. Some students said they would continue having children until they had a boy. In computing the averages, we assumed five children as a maximum for this group.

5. The census data for 1921-31 (Census of India, 1931:36-37) shows an increase of 7.4 percent for the Lewa Patidars and and 30 percent for the Barias. For 1931-41 (Census of India, 1941:79), the last census in which data are available by caste, an increase of 6.9 percent was shown for the Lewa Patidars and 39.2 percent for the Barias.

6. The Puranic ideal of redemption for women through obedience to and the service of their husbands.

References

Agarwala, S. N. "Raising the Marriage Age for Women: A Means to Lower the Birth Rate." Economic and Political Weekly (1966, 1):797-798.

Anker, R. "Socio-economic Determinants of Reproductive Behavior in Households of Rural Gujarat, India." Ph.D. Dissertation, University of Michigan, 1973.

Boulding, K. E. Review of M. Mamdani's The Myth of Population Control. New Republic, 168 (1973):22-23.

Chandrasekhar, S. "India's Family Planning Programme: What We Have Accomplished So Far." In Sixth All-India Conference on Family Planning. Bombay: Family Planning Association of India, 1968.

Freedman, R. and Berelson, B. "The Record of Family Planning Programs." Studies in Family Planning, 7, 1 (January 1976).

Government of Baroda. Census of India, 1911, v. 7. Baroda State Press.

Government of Baroda. Census of India, 1931, v. 19. Baroda State Press.

Government of Gujarat. Annual Administrative Report, Public Health Department, 1966. Ahmedabad, 1970.

Government of India Census, 1961. District Census Handbook 14 (Gujarat State, Baroda District).

Government of India Census, 1971. "Paper 1" in Series 1— India.

Gutherie, G. M. "The Psychology of Modernization in the Rural Philippines." Institute of Philippine Culture Papers, 8 (1971).

Hill, R.; Stycos, J. M.; and Back, K. W. The Family and Population Control. New Haven: College and University Press, 1959.

Hogel, H. "The Influence of Agricultural Extension in Selected Villages of Kaira District (Gujarat, India)." University of Michigan Comaparative Education Dissertation Series, 21 (1972).

Jain, S. P. "State of Growth Rates and Their Components." In A. Bose, ed., Patterns of Population Change in India. Calcutta: Allied Publishers, 1967.

Kapadia, K. M. Marriage and Family in India. Bombay: Oxford University Press, 1966.

Kuppuswamy, B.; Rao, K. S.; and Kanth, A. K., eds. Population Education. Bombay: Asia Publishing House, 1971.

Mamdani, M. The Myth of Population Control. New York: Monthly Review Press, 1972.

Mandelbaum, D. G. Human Fertility in India: Social Components and Policy Perspectives. Berkeley: University of California Press, 1975.

Mani, S. B. "Family Planning Communication in Rural India." Ph.D. Dissertation, Syracuse University.

McNamara, R. S. Annual Report of the World Bank, 1971.

Mehta, M. J. "A Study of the Practice of Female Infanticide among the Kambis of Gujarat." Journal of the Gujarat Research Society, 28 (1966):57-66.

Nag, M. "Factors Affecting Human Fertility in Nonindustrial Societies: A Cross-Cultural Study." Yale University Publications in Anthropology, 66 (1968). (Reprinted by Human Relations Area Files Press.)

Nair, K. Blossoms in the Dust. London: Duckworth, 1961.

Nortman, D. and Hofstatter, E. "Population and Family Planning Programs: A Factbook." Reports on Population/ Family Planning, 2 (1975).

Poffenberger, T. "Motivational Aspects of Resistance to Family Planning in an Indian Village." Demography, 5 (1968): 757-766.

Poffenberger, T. and Poffenberger, S. B. "The Social Psychology of Fertility Behavior in a Village in India." In J. T. Fawcett, ed., Psychological Perspectives on Population. New York: Basic Books, Inc., 1973:135-162.

Poffenberger, T. and Sebaly, K. "Population Learning among Secondary School Students in an Indian Village." Ann Arbor: Center for Population Planning, Mimeographed Monograph, May 1971.

Population Reference Bureau, Inda. "Ready or Not, Here They Come." Population Bulletin, 26 (1970).

Soni, V. India's Family Planning Programme. New Delhi: The Ford Foundation, 1971.

Stycos, J. M. "Demographic Chic at the UN." Family Planning Perspectives, 6 (1974):160-164.

Talwar, P. P. "Adocescent Sterility in an Indian Population." Human Biology, 37 (1965):256, 261.

Wyon, J. B. and Gordon, J. E. The Khanna Study: Population Problems in the Rural Punjab. Cambridge: Harvard University Press, 1971.

MPS 3   Norman G. Owen, ed. Compadre Colonialism. Studies on the Philippines under American Rule. Illustration, tables, bibliography. 318, paper.

MPS 4   Frank Shulman. Doctoral Dissertations on South Asia, 1966-1970. Appendices, indexes. xvii, 228, paper.

MPS 5   Harley Harris Bartlett. The Labors of the Datoe and Other Essays on the Bataks of Asahan (North Sumatra). Illustrations. xxiv, 387, paper.

MPS 6   John Stephen Lansing. Evil in the Morning of the World: Phenomenological Approaches to a Balinese Community. Illustration, bibliography. x, 104, paper.

MPS 7   Thomas R. Trautmann, ed. Kinship and History in South Asia. Diagrams. ix, 157, paper.

MPS 8   William P. Malm and Amin Sweeney. Studies in Malaysian Oral and Musical Traditions. Illustrations. x, 104, paper.

MPS 9   David M. Engel. Law and Kingship in Thailand during the Reign of King Chulalongkorn. Bibliography. x, 131, paper.

MPS 10   Thomas Poffenberger. Fertility and Family Life in an Indian Village. Tables. 108, paper.

Sp 1   Thomas Powers. Balita Mula Maynila (News from Manila). Illustrations. 40, paper.

LL 1   Peter Edwin Hook. The Compound Verb in Hindi. Index, bibliography. 318, paper.

LL 2   Madhav Deshpande. Critical Studies in Indian Grammarians I: The Theory of Homogeneity [Sāvarṇya]. Bibliography. xiii, 223, paper.

LL 3   Mary S. Zurbuchen. Introduction to Old Javanese Language and Literature: A Kawi Prose Anthology. Glossary, bibliography. xii, 150, paper.

CSSEAS Publications
130 Lane Hall
The University of Michigan
Ann Arbor, Mich. 48109